DOWN HOME WITH
THE NEELYS

A SOUTHERN FAMILY COOKBOOK

Patrick Neely and Gina Neely

With Paula Disbrowe

Photographs by Shelly Strazis

ALFRED A. KNOPF
New York
2009

THIS IS A BORZOI BOOK
PUBLISHED BY ALFRED A. KNOPF

Copyright © 2009 by Patrick Neely and Gina Neely

Photographs copyright © 2009 by Shelly Strazis

Foreword copyright © 2009 by Paula Deen

All rights reserved. Published in the United States by Alfred A. Knopf,
a division of Random House, Inc., New York,
and in Canada by Random House of Canada Limited, Toronto.

www.aaknopf.com

Knopf, Borzoi Books, and the colophon are registered trademarks of Random House, Inc.

Designed by Maggie Hinders

Library of Congress Cataloging-in-Publication Data
Neely, Patrick.
Down home with the Neelys : a Southern family cookbook / Patrick Neely and
Gina Neely, with Paula Disbrowe.
p.   cm.
Includes index.
ISBN 978-0-307-26994-2
1. Cookery, American—Southern style. 2. Barbecue cookery. I. Neely, Gina.
II. Disbrowe, Paula. III. Title.
TX715.2.S68N434   2009
641.5975—dc22   2008054393

Manufactured in the United States of America
Published May 12, 2009
Second Printing, October 2009

DOWN HOME WITH
THE NEELYS

Women hold up the world in so many ways, and that is why God blessed me with daughters. For Spenser and Shelbi, who taught me the meaning of unconditional love. Girls, go dream your dreams!

Love, Mom

Very few men are as lucky as I am to have three gorgeous ladies in his life. Gina, Spenser, and Shelbi, this is for YOU.

Pat

ecue fans who've asked get their wish: The Neelys (from left, Gaelin, Patrick, Tony, Mark) are opening a

NTERPRISE

Neely's BBQ branching out

By Byron McCauley
The Commercial Appeal

eely's Barbeque Restaurant plans to n a second location at 5700 Mt. Mori-

ext month's expansion is the first Neely's, which is owned and operat- by brothers Gaelin, Tony, Patrick Mark Neely.

hey are disciples of their uncle, Jim ely, who introduced the family to the becue business in 1978 when he ned Interstate Barbecue at 2265 S. rd. "He's always been in our cor- ," said Tony Neely, 33. "We just love 1 to death."

he Neely brothers opened Neely's in 8 on Madison Avenue and now oper- the restaurant at 670 Jefferson.

nitially that's pretty much all we

wanted to do," said Tony. "Basically, you've got four brothers working pretty much shoulder-to-shoulder" in one restaurant.

The second store provides a management challenge for the family, he said.

Tony and Mark, 29, will operate the new store. Patrick, 28, and Gaelin, 35, will continue to run the Jefferson restaurant.

Neely's will join a host of other restaurants in the busy area near Hickory Ridge Mall. Tony Neely said his customers for a long time had been asking about a second location out east, where many of them live. Many customers are hospital workers and downtown employees, he said.

"For about three years our customers have been telling us 'We wish you were out here,' " Tony Neely said.

Tony Neely is pleased with the heavi-

ly traveled site that he's be for more than a year, he said

"We've never had a place th so much drive-by traffic. We actually going to enhance bo he said. Tony Neely expects pany's catering business to ex serving customers east of L nue from the new store and v mar from the existing store.

The Neelys will spend abo to make the 4,800-square-foo like the Jefferson Avenue N will hire 25 to 30 people ini year, the restaurant will hav employees, Tony Neely said. T rant will seat 160 to 180 peop

"We are trying to build a s the restaurant," Tony Neely want them to come out here a same feel and say, 'This i We're home.' "

Contents

Foreword by Paula Deen

WHEN MY BOYS, BOBBY AND JAMIE, rolled into Nashville a couple years ago, looking for great food to feature on their show, *Road Tasted,* they struck it rich. They not only discovered fabulous barbecued ribs and pulled pork and barbecue spaghetti and baked beans at Neely's Bar-B-Que—they discovered Patrick and Gina Neely. I think the story went something like this: When my boys sat down to film the segment, they discovered that Pat was a gem, the kind of guy they'd want to hang out and have a few beers with. In between takes, they also found out that Gina was no shrinking violet and as spicy as the hot sauce they were shaking all over those ribs. Soon enough, the four of them were laughing and carrying on so much they practically forgot about the cameras. Then, like good boys, Bobby and Jamie called their momma and said, "I think we've found something really special here."

Indeed they had. Patrick and Gina Neely are not just extraordinary restaurateurs (they have restaurants in Nashville and Memphis) who have spent years in the trenches (like all of us in the business) serving great food, they are also warm and wonderful people and that rare thing, a husband and wife who actually work and cook together. And I'll be damned if they don't get along awfully well to boot. What's more, they have had the good sense to pay attention to the cooking of their parents and grandparents, and are passing on those traditions to their darling daughters, Spenser and Shelbi. That's what I call "gettin' it."

Before long, I had to get the Neelys to Savannah to see what all the fuss was about. I hosted them on *Paula's Party,* to which they brought most of their kin, and then things really got out of hand. As we all got to know each other, we realized we had much more in common than Southern food. In fact, their family mirrors mine in many ways—both the Neelys and the Deens faced challenges growing up, including losing parents at an early age. And both clans knew the value of hard work and the joy associated with providing something better for our children. Did I mention we also like to eat?

When my television producer and dear friend, Gordon Elliott, met the Neelys, he was instantly smitten. Mark Schneider, Gordon's partner at Follow Productions, flew to Memphis to see the Neelys in action and immediately called Gordon and said he'd found "the perfect couple" to star in a television series of their own. I wasn't the least bit surprised. And that's how *Down Home with the Neelys* was born.

Pat and Gina didn't go looking for television—it found them. Thank goodness! Now we all get to share in the warmth and laughter and good food that inspired *Down Home with the Neelys* the television series, and now this lovely cookbook. With the following recipes, we are all given a place at the Neely family table, and it's a seat I would take any day of the week. So what are y'all waiting for? Turn the page and dig in. Their recipes and heartwarming family anecdotes will fill your stomach full.

Savannah, July 2008

DOWN HOME WITH
THE NEELYS

GINA: We started out as friends, but I knew that wouldn't last, because I was **attracted** to that man.

Gina's Introduction

HEY, EVERYONE,

First of all, I want to thank you for reading our book and watching our show. We had no idea what we were getting into when we let television cameras into our house, but—you know what?—it's been fun. The show has allowed us to share our recipes with a lot of people, many of whom now come and visit us at the restaurants. It's also allowed us to tell some of our story.

We decided to put it all down on paper because folks kept asking. They'd send us letters, asking for our recipes. They'd send us e-mails, asking how we met. So we figured, give the public what they want. And that's pretty much how *Down Home* (the book) was born.

Pat and I have known each other a long, long time. I still remember the day we met, how awkward it was for the two of us. I mean, there was a spark for sure, but we were teenagers standing in a high-school hallway, and we really didn't know what to say (hint for you guys out there: start with *"Hello!"*). I think I finally broke the ice, and then Pat asked me for my number.

We started out as friends, but I knew that wouldn't last, because I was *attracted* to that man. I also knew the feeling was mutual. So we began dating. Dating brought the usual ups, downs, and separations, but as fate would have it, we were both grown up and single when we renewed our acquaintance. This time, we decided to marry. With such a long history, you'd think I knew what I was getting into. I had *no idea* what I was getting into, girl. But I was about to find out.

If you really want to get to know your spouse or partner, go into business with him. You'll see all his colors, which is what happened with Pat and me. I learned a lot about Pat and his family.

The Neelys work, laugh, love, and play harder than any family I have ever met. Their path has not been an easy one, which makes their success even more extraordinary. They are a tight-knit clan, and I had to fight for my place in this raucous group of five brothers, one sister, and one protective mother hen. I did it with Pat's help—indeed, with help from the entire Neely family.

I learned about commitment from the Neelys. I learned about dedication. And I learned about loyalty. The Neelys do not walk away from anything. If there's a problem, they fix it. If there's a spat, they make up. And if someone is in trouble, they'll drop what they're doing to lend a hand.

The family hanging out at home. TOP ROW: Tony, Jackie, Gaelin; BOTTOM ROW: Pat, Mark holding Cousin Jason, Chris

Pat has been there for me since day one. As a couple, we've been through good times and bad. As a person, I've had my doubts (I know you might not believe it, watching the show, but they've been there, trust me). All I can say is, if not for God, Pat, and my family standing beside me, Lord knows where I'd be.

The Neelys let me be me. They gave me confidence. They encouraged my participation in their business. Their confidence in me fed my creativity, creativity I used to help them grow their business. It was all working, going great, but we never imagined what would come next: Some crazy person wanted to put us on television!

We had no idea that our business partnership would serve as preparation for the work we now do on television, but it has. Working with Pat in the restaurant business has been the perfect apprenticeship. We have always loved what we do. It's not so much a job as a joyous calling. Joy is what we feel on the set when Pat forgets the camera is rolling (I'm always telling him, "This is a family show, hon!"). Joy is what we feel in preparing food for our restaurant customers, many of whom have become friends. And joy is what I feel when I sit down with the Neelys and see how much pleasure they take in making sure their loved ones are happy and well fed.

It is our hope that this book will deliver some of that joy, and give you a sense of how it feels to eat at our table.

And just in case Pat missed how I've been feeling all these years, here it is, babe, in writing: You helped me become the woman I always dreamed of being!

Thank you, Pat. Thank you, everyone. Now, eat up! Oink!

Love,
GINA NEELY

PAT: Gina had my heart, and it didn't take long
before she had my stomach, too.

Pat's Introduction

HELLO, FOLKS,

I'll start this book out by agreeing with my wife, Gina (this is a habit of mine—it keeps me out of trouble). Gina and I could not be more surprised, pleased, or blessed by the fact that the long and smoky road that is our life in the barbecue business has led to hosting our own television show and now sharing this, our first book, with you. But, boy oh boy, has it been fun. And although we're still adjusting to living out of a suitcase, the success we have enjoyed, and continue to enjoy, really isn't very complicated. For the Neely family, our story begins with the food. One of the reasons we are so connected as a family is our long tradition of cooking and eating together. And as you're about to discover, it got us through a lot.

My dad with Gaelin and Tony shopping during the holidays

In some ways, I've always felt that we weren't meant to be here—the Neely family, that is. My late father, William Neely, was born prematurely and was so small, according to his sisters, Faye and Delores, that he slept in a doll's box. Now, this was the 1930s, and a midwife delivered him—can you imagine how scary that was? More heartache was to follow: The birth was such a strain on his mother that she died three days later of pneumonia.

My father's challenges continued. He was born with sickle-cell anemia, so, although he loved sports, he couldn't play them. I can't help thinking: this guy just wasn't supposed to make it. But my dad did make it. He went on to live his life, marry my mother, Lorine, and father six children—the five brothers,

Our Jefferson Avenue Midtown location

Gaelin, Tony, Mark, me, and Christopher, and one sister, Jackie. He did his best to provide for us. Then, when he was forty years old, my dad died suddenly and unexpectedly. I was eleven years old.

After he died, finances became a constant worry in our household. My mother worked very hard to support us, and keep us well fed, but it was tough. I will never forget the day I came home to find the power cut off in our house because she couldn't pay the electric bill. That moment had a big impact on all of us. I remember wanting to do everything I could to help my family and create something for myself.

When I was in high school, our uncle Jim Neely opened a small barbecue restaurant. Uncle Jim provided jobs for his extended family, and before long we were all working for him. In fact, during my senior year of high school, even though I played football, I worked for him seven days a week. You could say I developed a strong work ethic early on, out of necessity. As teenagers, we all wanted spending money, of course, and I had dreams of getting a car, but we also needed to help our momma out. When I was in college, Mom actually

February 28, 1988, the night before Neely's opened. Notice there's no stove, just a two-eye burner.

lost her home because of a foreclosure. This was devastating. I had no choice but to come back to Memphis.

So my brother Tony and I went back to work for my uncle. We shared a small house behind his restaurant as part of our compensation. Tony and I leaned on each other a lot during those years, and dreamed about opening a place of our own.

We fell in love with the chaos and hard work of the restaurant business. The smell of hickory wood, charcoal, and meat cooking on the grill became a passion, and by the time we were in our twenties, the art of slow-cooking Southern barbecue was in our blood. We decided to follow in Uncle Jim's footsteps and open a barbecue joint of our own.

By then, we knew a thing or two about barbecue. We knew that seasoning meat with a spice mix—or "dry rub," as it's called in Memphis—coaxed out the best flavor, and that slow-cooking with indirect heat provided the juiciest results. But we didn't know much about the business side of running restaurants, so, to further our knowledge, Tony and I enrolled in an intensive

The Neely brothers, Mark, Pat, Tony, and Gaelin, standing in front of the Jefferson Avenue restaurant

two-year management-training program with the McDonald's Corporation. When we completed the course, we had the confidence to break out on our own.

Though our restaurant dreams were big, our finances were small—and there were plenty of naysayers who doubted our chances, based on our age and lack of capital. Luckily, our ninety-year-old grandmother, Rena, believed in our dream. She had enough faith in our enterprise to loan us $20,000, using her home as collateral. It's a gesture that we will never, ever forget. And that's pretty much how Neely's Bar-B-Que was conceived.

My brothers Mark and Gaelin were immediately on board. We were all eager to get started, but there were still plenty of obstacles to overcome. Generous as it was, the $20,000 from dear Momma Rena wasn't nearly enough to open a restaurant in 1988. But eventually things fell into place. We secured a two-thousand-square-foot space at 694 Madison Avenue, in downtown Memphis, and converted it into a restaurant. We did all of the renovation ourselves. We couldn't afford fry vats or a stove, so we used a simple two-eye electric burner to simmer our sauces.

We had just enough money left for a few tables and chairs and, most important, a barbecue pit. The paint had barely dried on the walls when the health inspector arrived. Minutes before we were set to open, we got the green light. Somehow, without a cash register or a walk-in cooler, we celebrated the grand opening of our first Neely's Bar-B-Que restaurant on February 29, 1988—a leap year. We kept the money from our first several days of sales in a shoebox.

The actual menu was the least of our worries. After all our years sweating in the kitchen—and over the fire—we were confident about our technique and signature approach to Memphis-style pork and beef ribs, as well as such side dishes as Molasses-Baked Beans and Sweet and Spicy Slaw, along with a few irresistible desserts, like peach cobbler and Sock-It-to-Me Cake. Within a few months, and particularly after a local food critic known for ripping restaurants apart stopped by (unannounced) and gave us an enthusi-

astic review, business was booming. Soon we were able to afford a cash register, a walk-in cooler, and the other necessities to handle the lines around the corner at lunch.

After just two years, we had paid back Momma Rena and saved $40,000,

Momma Neely joins the family business.

enough to purchase the building at 670 Jefferson Avenue and move into our current location. In 1992, we bought a second property, for an outpost in East Memphis. I think it's significant that we brothers were able to start a successful business within just a few years of starting out with only $20,000.

With our second restaurant, we knew we needed to rely on more family members to help get things done. So, as soon as the business could afford it, we asked our mother to retire from her banking job and come work for us. Momma was more than happy to do so; she had worked all those years and *never* earned enough money to pay all her bills. Well, now her hard work finally paid off: We gave her a huge retirement party at Neely's. These days, Mom visits both Memphis locations twice a week, to bake cakes and supervise our desserts.

The Neely picture was finally complete when my wife and partner, Gina, came on board. She not only rocked my world (more on that later), she rocked our business as she took on catering, customer relations, and recipe development. Gina and my momma brought a new energy to the restaurants, and helped take our business to another level. The tremendous success we began to enjoy was largely attributable to them.

On top of that, the accolades started pouring in. In 1997, Neely's won a contest held by a local television station for the "best ribs in Memphis." After that, Tony and I were featured on the *Today* show with Al Roker. Over the years, we've become buddies with Al and had some memorable meals with him. Now, whenever there's someone in the *Today* show's audience from Memphis, he says, "Be sure to say hi to the Neelys for me."

Our business continued to thrive, and in March 2001, we opened a third location, in Nashville. Tony relocated to run that restaurant. Today we operate five concessions in the FedExForum, home of the NBA Memphis Grizzlies, and we plan to keep growing.

We had no idea, on that first day more than twenty years ago, that Neely's would become a barbecue powerhouse in Memphis (a city that many consider to be the barbecue capital of the country), and we couldn't be prouder of the praise our restaurants have earned. And never in our wildest dreams did Gina and I imagine that we would have our own cooking show! Things sure have changed since we started. But what hasn't changed is our work ethic.

My sweetheart brought a powerful presence to the entire operation.

On one level, the success we have enjoyed isn't very complicated, and it starts with the food. When my brothers and sister and I were growing up, meals were one of the main things that drew us together, and this came from both sides of the family. My mother learned to cook from her extended family, and she tried to please my father by cooking recipes from his side of the family as well. Now I cook recipes from both families for my children.

Then, lo and behold, I met a woman who has the same connections to food and family. Gina learned to cook from Nana (her godmother), her great-grandma Callie, and her mother, Jean. Our marriage brought those histories and traditions together, and that has been a springboard to our family restau-

Our original location was small, but our dreams were huge.

rants and national TV shows. Indeed, the joys of simple food and down-home cooking have stood us well.

Given our rough beginning, you might say that *we* weren't supposed to make it, either. But here we are, three decades after my father's death, getting it done. William Neely's kids are running several restaurants and raising beautiful children, and Gina and I are hosting a national television show. If he had not made it, our story would never have been told. My dad was a proud man, and I like to think that he's up there watching all this, nudging the angels and saying, "Look at my boys; I told you they'd do something good." This book is for him, and for all the Neelys.

The Reunion: Pat and Gina's Sizzlin' Love

Pat: There are two things in Memphis that take time (and patience!): making love and making barbecue. In my lifetime, I've discovered that both are worth the wait.

I was fifteen when I met the love of my life, and I'll remember that moment forever. It was the first day of my sophomore year in high school. My mother and my brother Mark and I were attending an open house at Melrose High School, and the hall was jammed with parents and students. As we walked down the hallway to find my homeroom teacher, my eyes locked on a gorgeous young lady. She was wearing a neat blouse and skirt and standing with an older woman. As we got closer, my mother said, "Hey, girl, how you been? It's been so long since I've seen you!" Then she hugged the older woman, and they started to talk. It took my mom forever to introduce Mark and me. "These are my boys Mark and Patrick," she finally said. To which the woman, Jean, replied, "And this is my daughter Gina." I was dazed. I don't believe I opened my mouth. I couldn't take my eyes off her. I'm sure Gina was thinking, "Can he talk?"

My girl has always had a beautiful smile.

When we walked away, I asked my mother, "Who was that?" She replied, "Aw, that's Jean. We went to school here decades ago, and we graduated together." "Mom," I said, "I'm not talking about that old lady, I'm talking about the girl." My mom gave me a look and said, "That's her daughter." She added that I had better make damn sure I paid as much attention to my schoolwork!

Over the next year, I would gaze at this stunning beauty every chance I got. Of course, she never looked my way—she was dating a junior, and I was a dumb, young sophomore. But I didn't care, and one day I finally got the courage to ask Gina for her phone number, and she was nice enough to give it to me. We began to talk on the phone, and, unbelievably, she would occasionally call me! The more we talked, the more I tried to find things about her I disliked (surely there must be a catch!), but I couldn't find any. So we became friends.

When we started our junior year, we were still just friends. I was becoming a good football player, and between practice, games, schoolwork, and work-

Pat, after winning a football game

ing at my uncle's barbecue restaurant, there wasn't much time for anything else (though I did spend an awful lot of time *thinking* about Gina). The summer before my senior year, I called her one day and found out she was in the hospital, having emergency surgery to remove her appendix. I borrowed my brother's car and drove out to the hospital to visit her. By the time I got there, she had already had the surgery. She was in the recovery room, and I asked her mother if I could see her. When I went into her room, she was lying on her back, feeling awful but looking as gorgeous as ever. When she opened her eyes, I could tell she was shocked that this seventeen-year-old boy cared enough to drive all the way out there to see her. I knew if this wasn't enough to steal her heart nothing would.

For the next few weeks, I would walk from Melrose to Cella Street, where Gina lived, and visit her after football practice. I'd bring along anything I thought would brighten her day or make her feel better. We would sit on the sofa and talk, and I knew that something was changing in our relationship. During one visit, she was wearing a yellow sundress, and had her stunning brown legs oiled up. She also had on lip gloss. The whole package was incredibly tantalizing. I finally said to myself, "You better make your move." Holding her hand, I leaned over and closed my eyes, unsure whether she would reject or accept my offer. Well, guess what—she came closer to me, and we kissed! I

left in a daze. I had dated before, but no one had ever dazzled me like this. I was heading into my senior year, I was a first-string football player, and I had just kissed a girl who made my knees buckle and my stomach feel like Jell-O. Things were pretty good.

Gina as a junior in high school, the year she became my girl

When we started our senior year, it was official that Gina was my girl. She came to my football games on Friday nights and ate dinner at my house on Sundays. After football season, I began to work a lot more at my uncle's restaurant—every evening after school, and on weekends. This schedule would be challenging to any relationship, let alone a young, fumbling high-school one. For a time, Gina would come to my uncle's place on Sundays, when it was slow, and sit with me for hours. But finally my schedule took its toll on us. This was just before the spring prom, and we never made it there as a couple. We graduated and parted ways—I went off to college to pursue my football dreams, and Gina moved to California to live with her older sister and attend college. We both married other people. Life moved on, but deep down I was heartbroken.

Over the next ten years, I would often think about Gina. When I saw her mother, Ms. Jean, I would ask about her. And when Gina came to Memphis to visit and we ran into each other, I felt the same way I had the first time I saw her in the hallway at Melrose High.

When it was time for our ten-year high-school reunion, my family's first restaurant was open, and it became a local contact for classmates to call. One day, while working in the kitchen, I took a call and I immediately recognized that soft, sexy voice on the other end of the phone. My legs got weak, my body felt warm, and I knew my feelings for Gina hadn't changed one bit. We must have talked for over an hour. She told me she was planning to return for the reunion—and that she was newly single. So was I. I became very excited.

Let me tell you, our reunion was a *real reunion*. The banquet was the prom we never had. We decided to attend together, and the flame was instantly rekindled. Gina was just as I remembered her: petite, sexy, and very neat, with a stunning, confident walk.

When Gina decided to move back to Memphis after the reunion, all my prayers were answered. She moved into a small house, and I visited often. I just couldn't get enough of her. I had my own barbecue business, and I was dating the girl of my dreams. Life was almost perfect.

Gina had a darling daughter, Spenser, from her previous marriage, whom I simply adored. Gina also had my heart, and it didn't take long before she had my stomach, too. What was surprising to me was how well this amazing woman could *cook*. Whenever I visited, she always had something simmering on the stove or baking in the oven—smoky collard greens, barbecue meatloaf, macaroni and cheese, chocolate-marshmallow brownies—all the good Southern dishes my mother cooked, and more. I was never a fan of collards (my mother always cooked turnip greens), but when Gina put a plate of them in front of me and I ate them, I forgot all about turnip greens. I asked her how she'd learned to cook. She told me she actually didn't get around to cooking until she left home and missed good Southern cooking. So she would call her mother, her great-grandmother, and her godmother, Nana (God bless those women!), in the South to get their recipes, and then she started cooking.

We were happy. We were in love. And we were cooking together! I made Gina late-night feasts of spicy chicken wings and more.

After years of waiting, I was finally able to put a wedding ring on her finger.

It didn't take me long to realize that I wasn't about to let Gina get away from me again. I proposed, she accepted, and we were married on July 5, 1995. It was one of the happiest and most exciting days of my life. Life was good, and it wasn't long before Shelbi, our second daughter, was born. In the years that followed, Gina and I spent many evenings at home together cooking. As our children grew, we took turns preparing memorable dishes for them as well as for extended family on holidays and special occasions. Of the many, many things Gina and I have in common, cooking and enjoying great food is at the top of the list. We tried to capture that spirit in this book, and it is our hope that you'll have as much fun preparing these recipes as we did putting them down on paper.

Neely Knowledge

Pat: The food in this book is born of three generations of Neelys. Over the years, we have developed a few preferences and kitchen habits that have become second nature in our cooking. What follows is our list of staple ingredients, along with six recipes that are key to eating like a Neely.

First things first: To be a true and legitimate Memphis barbecue restaurant, you need a signature sauce and seasoning. It's our holy grail, baby, and without it your ribs won't sing. My brother Tony took on this project with gusto. After two years of testing and tasting, we hit the mother lode, developing sauce and seasoning recipes that are, near as we can tell, absolute perfection. And now we are sharing them for the first time. You'll want to have big batches of both on hand as staples, because we use them as the base for countless recipes in this book. I've made the versions in this chapter at home, as well as in the pits at the restaurant, with equally delicious results. With the following recipes, and the cooking tips that we provide for each one, you'll amaze your friends and family with your backyard pit-master skills! Finally, at the Neely table, no family meal is complete without gravy—and plenty of it. My mother's method for making gravy—one that she learned from her mother—is the only gravy recipe you'll ever need.

How proud I was to be catering our first event.

SALT: We use kosher. It comes in a big blue box at the supermarket. Kosher salt has a much larger crystal size than table salt, and generally imparts a cleaner flavor to whatever you're cooking. Kosher salt crystals are so big that they will not fit through a traditional saltshaker (we use a Parmesan cheese shaker instead). We also keep a small bowl of the stuff by the stove, and dip in with our fingers whenever a dish needs a little more salty goodness.

BLACK PEPPER: There's no substitute for freshly ground black pepper. If you don't have a pepper mill, go out and get one. You'll thank us later. There are a variety of whole black peppercorns to choose from, and they are available at supermarkets and through a number of mail-order sources (Penzeys is one of our favorites).

VEGETABLES: They should be washed, trimmed, and peeled when necessary.

FLOUR: Use all-purpose unless otherwise specified.

BUTTER: We prefer unsalted for everything.

EGGS: Use large; this is particularly important for baking.

PEPPERS AND CHILES: They should be stemmed and seeded unless otherwise specified.

BAY LEAVES: We use whole dried bay leaves. The most important thing to remember about bay leaves is to remove them from the dish before you serve it.

HOT SAUCE: When we first started cooking there was only one hot sauce in our pantry, and that was Louisiana brand (it's still our favorite). Since then, hot sauce has become a hot commodity, and there are literally hundreds of sauces to choose from. There are even hot sauce websites and blogs! Now, if you're a Neely, that's the kind of progress you like to see.

CREOLE MUSTARD: When it comes to mustard, we like ours with a little heat. Creole is a great choice because it provides heat with a horseradishy kick, something you won't find in other mustards.

SCALLIONS: They should be fresh and firm, with a little snap in the stem. We trim both ends and use the white and light green parts.

Neely's Barbecue Seasoning

In the South, we have a tradition of ushering recipes from era to era and family to family. Secret sauces are passed down from generation to generation. That's certainly the case here. Our Barbecue Seasoning and Barbecue Sauce have evolved over time, and the versions that follow have benefited from the contributions of countless kin through the years.

Now that we are passing our family secrets along to you, it's your job to share them with others. We enjoy changing up recipes and seeing what happens, and we encourage you to do the same. Who knows? You may come up with a secret sauce or rub that's better than our own!

Of course, the keys to full-flavored barbecue—indeed, one of the keys to any great-tasting dish—are fresh ingredients and spices. Don't be reaching in the back of the cupboard for some tired old tin of paprika. You want great ribs? Start with fresh spices.

Everyone down South knows that a good grill seasoning (or "dry rub," as it's called in Memphis) begins with paprika. We use the basic paprika that is not labeled "sweet" or "hot." The flavor is subtly sweet, rich, and yet mild, so it blends beautifully with grilled meats. Sugar and onion powder provide a sweet and savory counterpoint.

Keep in mind that you will be cooking over charcoal and hickory (or your preferred wood), which will add tremendous flavor to the meat. For that reason, this seasoning blend is fairly simple and straightforward.

For the best flavor, marinate the spice-rubbed meats overnight in the refrigerator, so they can absorb and "breathe in" the flavors.

1½ cups paprika
¾ cup sugar
3¾ tablespoons onion powder

Stir together the ingredients in a small bowl. Stored in an airtight container in a cool, dry place, this seasoning will last for up to 6 months.

MAKES ABOUT 2½ CUPS

Neely's Barbecue Sauce

Pat: My brother Tony has a terrific palate, and his true genius is in having developed the right "tempo" for our barbecue sauce—and, boy oh boy, he never lets us forget it! This recipe, which includes Neely's Barbecue Seasoning and eleven other ingredients, became one of the keys to our success as restaurateurs. Now it can be the base of your own kitchen success.

Memphis barbecue sauce is known for its sweet and tangy tomato base. Ours keeps true to that tradition, striking a perfect balance between the sweet (we use brown and white sugar), the tangy (cider vinegar), and the tomato base (good ole ketchup!). Any self-respecting Memphis pit master will tell you that the sauce must complement the meat without overpowering it, and ours does just that.

At the restaurant we simmer the sauce for five hours, and we always taste the blend before cooking it, making sure we've got all the ingredients working. Over the years, we've learned that if it tastes good before it cooks, it's gonna be outstanding after a long, slow simmer. The end result: an insanely thick, rich, and sweet sauce, and the perfect adornment for any rack anywhere.

---

2 cups ketchup

1 cup water

1/4 cup light-brown sugar

1/4 cup granulated sugar

1 1/2 teaspoons freshly ground black pepper

1 1/2 teaspoons onion powder

1 1/2 teaspoons dry mustard powder

2 tablespoons fresh lemon juice

2 tablespoons Worcestershire sauce

1/2 cup apple-cider vinegar

2 tablespoons light corn syrup

1 tablespoon Neely's Barbecue Seasoning (page 22)

Combine all of the ingredients in a large pot or a Dutch oven. Bring to a boil over high heat, stirring frequently to prevent sticking. Reduce the temperature to very low and simmer, uncovered, for at least 2 hours, stirring occasionally. Remove from the heat, cool, and use as needed. Stored in a tightly sealed container, this sauce will keep in the fridge for up to 2 months.

MAKES ABOUT 2 CUPS

NOTE: We never salt our Barbecue Sauce because of the sodium content in the ketchup and because other ingredients like onion powder and Worcestershire sauce provide so much flavor. Since our sauce is mostly used on grilled items (that are seasoned) and combined with other foods (like Barbecue Spaghetti and Molasses-Baked Beans), we don't want to end up with food that is too salty. So we err on the side of slightly underseasoning this sauce (although believe me, no one *ever* says that it lacks flavor). If your taste buds yearn for a little more salt, you can season the sauce—at the end of the cooking time—as you please.

Lorine's Brown Flour Gravy

Pat: My mother, Lorine, loved spending time in the kitchen and started cooking when she was a young girl. Friends knew her as the girl in school who enjoyed taking home-economics classes and collecting recipes, and when they went looking for her they knew where to go (the kitchen). Cooking is something she has kept at her whole life, so it's no surprise that Momma has become the best gravy-maker in our family. What makes this recipe special is

Shelbi, Lorine, and Spenser

that Momma learned it from her mother. It's an heirloom, and you're gonna love it. Our family has never prepared "white" or cream gravies; we prefer what is called a brown flour gravy, meaning the flour is browned in fat before the liquid is added, which creates a particularly rich flavor.

This recipe is meant to be a guide. Feel free to adjust the fat, flour, and liquid according to the amount you want to prepare. But the proportions we give are dead-on, and will result in one of the most delicious gravies you will ever prepare. It's slammin' over mashed potatoes, pork roast, fried chicken, and Gina's Perfect Rice.

---

2 tablespoons rendered bacon fat
$\frac{1}{2}$ cup all-purpose flour
1 to 1$\frac{1}{2}$ cups water
1 medium onion, sliced into $\frac{1}{4}$-inch rings
Salt
Freshly ground black pepper
Lawry's Seasoned Salt

Heat the bacon fat in a cast-iron skillet over medium-low heat. When the fat has melted and begins to sizzle, sprinkle in the flour, and stir with a wooden spoon until it is absorbed. Continue stirring the flour (being careful that it doesn't burn; reduce the heat if necessary) until it turns the color of a brown paper sack. When the flour is brown and starting to bubble, stir in a cup of water (or 1$\frac{1}{2}$ cups if you want a thinner gravy). When the water is incorporated into the flour, add the onion, and salt, pepper, and Lawry's Seasoned Salt to taste. Simmer until the onion has softened and the gravy is thickened, 5 to 8 minutes.

MAKES ABOUT 1$\frac{1}{4}$ CUPS

Gina's Perfect Rice

Gina: In the South, rice is an essential partner for roast pork or chicken, or anything with a tomatoey sauce or gravy, but even down here, folks sometimes find themselves a little intimidated by the process of making it. If you are the least bit nervous about cooking rice, look no further than our recipe. It delivers foolproof results every time, cooking up fragrant, fluffy rice infused with aromatics (shallots, garlic, and a few fresh herbs).

---

2 tablespoons butter
1 shallot, finely chopped
1½ cups long-grain white rice
½ teaspoon kosher salt
Freshly ground black pepper to taste
2½ cups Chicken Stock (page 28) or
    water, warmed
2 sprigs fresh thyme
2 bay leaves
1 garlic clove, smashed
1 tablespoon chopped fresh flat-leaf
    parsley

Melt the butter in a 2-quart saucepan over medium heat. Add the shallot, and sauté until tender, 3 to 4 minutes. Add the rice, and stir until the rice is glossy and coated with the butter. Season the rice with the salt and some pepper, and then add the warmed stock, the sprigs of thyme, bay leaves, and smashed garlic clove. Bring the mixture to a simmer, cover the pot with a tight-fitting lid, reduce the heat to low, and cook for 15 to 17 minutes, until all of the liquid has been absorbed.

Remove the pan from the heat, and keep it covered for another 5 minutes. Remove the lid, take out the thyme, bay leaves, and garlic, and fluff the rice with a fork, adding the chopped parsley at the same time.

SERVES 4 TO 6

Chicken Stock

Gina: Homemade chicken stock is our way of adding a little extra love to any dish, from soup to stew to rice pilaf. And it's so easy to make: We throw a whole bird (yeah, the whole thing) in the soup pot, along with plenty of aromatics, and let it simmer for a few hours. This gives our stock plenty of taste. For an even richer chicken flavor, add the carcass of a roasted chicken to the stock as you are cooking it.

4 quarts cold water
One 3½- to 4-pound chicken, cut into
    8 pieces, plus neck and giblets
    (do not use the liver)
2 onions, quartered
1 celery stalk, coarsely chopped
2 carrots, coarsely chopped
2 garlic cloves, unpeeled
1 teaspoon kosher salt
6 fresh flat-leaf parsley sprigs
8 whole black peppercorns
½ teaspoon dried thyme, crumbled
2 to 3 dried bay leaves

Bring the cold water and the chicken pieces (including the neck and giblets) to a boil. Reduce the heat to low, and begin skimming the froth immediately. Continue to simmer the stock, uncovered, skimming froth occasionally, for 2½ hours. Add the onions, celery, carrots, garlic, salt, parsley, peppercorns, thyme, and bay leaves to the pot. Simmer for another hour (adding the veggies and spices at the end gives our stock a little extra snap).

Pour the stock through a fine-mesh sieve into a large bowl and discard the solids. If you are using the stock right away, skim off and discard any fat. If not, cool the stock completely, uncovered, before skimming off and discarding the fat (this will be easier to do when the stock is cool).

MAKES ABOUT 10 CUPS

NOTE: This stock will keep for 1 week in the refrigerator, or it can be frozen for up to 3 months.

Crusty Cornbread

Pat: A cast-iron skillet is, far and away, the best pan for cooking this cornbread. In fact, we don't prepare it in anything else. Preheating the skillet in the oven creates a crispy golden crust, and it really seems to help the batter pop up and rise beautifully during the baking process. We serve the warm cornbread straight from the skillet with a big ole wooden spoon.

2 cups all-purpose flour

2 cups finely ground yellow cornmeal

2 tablespoons sugar

2 teaspoons baking powder

2 teaspoons salt

2¼ cups milk

2 large eggs

6 tablespoons butter, melted and slightly cooled

1 tablespoon rendered bacon fat (or butter, shortening, or vegetable oil)

Preheat oven to 400°F. Place a 10-inch cast-iron skillet in the oven and heat for at least 30 minutes. Meanwhile, make the batter.

Whisk together the flour, cornmeal, sugar, baking powder, and salt in a large bowl. In a medium bowl, whisk together the milk, eggs, and melted butter.

Make a well in the center of the dry ingredients and pour the wet ingredients into the well. Use a fork or spatula to stir until evenly combined.

Remove the skillet from the oven, add the bacon fat to the skillet, and swirl to coat. Pour the batter into the skillet and, using a spatula, spread the batter evenly across the pan. Bake for 25 to 30 minutes, until lightly golden and firm and springy to the touch.

MAKES 6 TO 8 SERVINGS

NOTE: For a richer flavor, you can melt an additional 2 tablespoons of butter over the top of the cornbread when it comes out of the oven.

Hog Wild: Memphis-Style Barbecue

MEMPHIS, TENNESSEE, is best known for the blues that pour out of bars and restaurants along Beale Street, and for everything barbecue. Its oldest restaurants are legendary halls of smoke and sauce, and the Neelys are proud to be part of that tradition.

Tennessee has a long history of smoking pork. Pigs were a food staple in the pre–Civil War South. They were easy and economical to raise, and they could be put out to forage in the forest and caught when the food supply became low. These semi-feral pigs produced tougher meat than the grain-fed varieties of pork we enjoy today, so long, slow cooking was essential. Slow cooking, as barbecue aficionados know, tenderizes the meat. And anyone who appreciates fine barbecue knows that one of its magical qualities is the way it falls off the bone and melts in your mouth. These early cooks were resourceful by necessity and used every part of the pig. Pig slaughters were

celebrations, and the whole neighborhood would share in the feast. The festive nature of Southern barbecue grew out of this tradition.

By the beginning of the twentieth century, when the rural farmland of the South became more urban and industrialized, pork was rarely butchered at home. It was purchased at grocery stores, and as a result, restaurants took over the time-consuming task of slow-cooking pork. The early restaurants began as rustic pits; over time they added stools, walls, full menus, and eventually the ubiquitous happy pig caricatures that seem to adorn every other building in the South.

Memphis-style barbecue is distinctive in many ways. Unlike the vinegar-and-mustard-based sauces of the East Coast, the one Memphis is known for is a sweet, tangy, tomato-based sauce. Thanks to the city's location on the Mississippi, the early Memphis sauce-makers had a large repertoire of ingredients to work with. Molasses was shipped upriver, so it became a popular seasoning for the sauce, along with black pepper and paprika.

The other distinctive thing about Memphis barbecue is that it's either "wet" or "dry." For the former, the meat is basted with sauce as it cooks, and then served with more of it on the side when it's finished. For the latter, meats are rubbed with a dry mixture of seasonings before they're cooked. Sometimes meat is ordered wet *and* dry, and then it gets hit with both.

Memphis is most famous for pulled pork. The meat (typically a pork shoulder) is slow-cooked and then shredded by hand into moist, succulent threads to be doused in a tangy sauce. Pulled pork is most commonly enjoyed in a sandwich, on a soft bun with a layer of coleslaw. Memphis barbecue also encompasses slow-cooked beef and pork ribs, as well as chicken and turkey accompanied by sides of coleslaw, baked beans, cornbread, and sometimes French fries.

As you'll see in the following recipes, the Neelys have gone hog-wild with this tradition, using our signature dry rub and sauce to flavor a multitude of dishes, including spaghetti, pizza, nachos, and more.

Tony's Tips

I'LL COME RIGHT OUT and say it: Cooking is my life. I can't imagine doing anything else for a living. I never thought of myself as an artist (I'm more of a blue-collar kind of guy), but there is an artistry in cooking that I find incredibly satisfying. I start with a blank canvas and take it from there. A splash of this, a dash of that, and pretty soon I'm on to something tasty, and that's the key. I'm always thinking about how our customers and my family—they're my toughest customers!—might respond to a dish. Hearing them say that something is the best thing they've ever tasted is about the best feeling in the world. The only thing I can think of that's better is raising children.

GET THE RIGHT GRILL

When I was a kid, my grandfather grilled in a hole in the backyard. He'd dig a hole, pile bricks on either side, burn the coal directly on the ground, and place a grate over the hole. After that, the first "real" grill I ever saw was a drum grill. Back then, drum grills were simply recycled industrial containers with legs welded to them. In the South, you could buy these babies alongside the road. So while I am deeply rooted in these old-style methods of barbecuing, I sure am happy that things have gotten a lot easier for the backyard grill master. We use a Char-Griller Smokin Pro, which is a good, solid grill, but there are countless other options available.

Basically, it comes down to a personal preference: Are you a gas grill or a charcoal grill guy? If you're the latter, your options include little hibachis

Tony loves to cook with indirect heat. Here he is lining his firebox with charcoal and hickory wood.

(great for direct, high-heat grilling of kebabs and small cuts of meat), table grills (long, narrow grills for direct, high-heat cooking of steaks, chops, and seafood), and kettle and drum grills (the kettle being the classic deep-rounded bowl with a dome lid) that allow you to cover the food and cook it slower at a lower temperature—they're essential for Southern-style barbecue. Gas and charcoal grills are two entirely different animals. I think the preference is somewhat regional; you're likely to see a lot more gas grills up north, but in most backyards in the South you'll find charcoal grills, which are my personal preference. Regardless of which kind you choose, a grill with a thermometer is ideal, so you can maintain an even temperature.

A gas grill is essentially a metal box heated by liquid propane–fueled burners. The heating surface (lava stones, ceramic briquettes or tiles, or metal bars) is positioned above the burners. Propane has no flavor, but you can achieve a smoky nuance when juices and fat drip onto the heating surface, and by using wood chips. To use wood chips on a gas grill, simply place the soaked wood chips in a smoker box, pie tin, or loaf pan, and place the container directly over one of the burners. Heat over high heat until the chips begin to smolder, then reduce the heat to the desired temperature for barbecuing.

Modern gas grills have two or three cooking zones, so you can play with the controls to create direct (over high heat) or indirect (using medium heat) grilling. For indirect grilling, all you need to do is reduce or turn off the heat directly underneath the meat. If your grill has three burners, you simply turn off the center burner and cook the meat in the center.

Both gas and charcoal grills have their pros and cons. Gas grills are so convenient; after a long day of work it's nice to turn a switch and have a grill going. They're also fairly foolproof because they allow you to maintain an even, consistent temperature. But they lack the "live fire" excitement and sensory pleasures of charcoal grilling. Charcoal requires a bit more time and artistry to maintain the temperature (that's the fun part), but it produces a one-of-a-kind smoky flavor.

I'm not terribly finicky about what kind of grates to use for a grill. Simply choose grates that feel solid and are easy to raise and lower so you can adjust them for cooking different kinds of meat and fish. For instance, I'll cook a nice, thick steak down low, directly over the heat, but I'll smoke a piece of salmon up high, over a gentle heat. (You can also regulate heat with higher piles of charcoal, or by raising or lowering the temperature on a gas grill, but it's easier, and more reliable, to be able to move the food closer or farther away from the heat source.)

The other consideration when choosing grates is how easy they are to clean (for example, choose grates with large, straight bar racks made of cast iron, as opposed to cheap, thin, likely-to-rust metal crosshatch bars). Clean grates mean healthier grilling and a purer taste, because there will be less buildup of charred debris. I like to clean my grates when they are still warm. I put on heavy, heat-resistant gloves, spray the grates with a mixture of water and degreaser (available at Home Depot or Lowe's), and scrub them down with a good wire brush.

Look for a grill with at least two racks, a lower one for meat and a higher, shorter one for corn on the cob, bell peppers, and other vegetables.

A rotisserie is not essential, but it is a luxury to have, because it rotates the meat to create an evenly browned texture. The (slight) downside is that it's a mechanical item that requires oil and upkeep.

HARDWOODS FOR SMOKIN'

Wood chips (or chunks) are the best way to produce a smoky flavor when cooking on either a gas or a charcoal grill. My favorite is hickory—it's the classic choice for Memphis-style barbecuing, and it was *made* for pork. Hickory is slow burning and has a smooth, rich flavor. I also love pecan and all the fruitwoods (such as apple and cherry) for pork and chicken. If apple wood were more plentiful in the South, I'd use it all the time. Mesquite wood is very popular in Texas, but I find that it has a strong, pungent flavor—which goes against our barbecue philosophy. If we wanted such a pronounced flavor, we'd use more charcoal. Patrick and I prefer a more subtle smoke, which is why our favorites are hickory, apple, and pecan. If you like the robust flavor of mesquite, keep in mind that it's best for beef.

Never use plywood or pressure-treated lumber, because there's a chance it's been treated with toxic chemicals.

Wood chips don't need much soaking time. You don't want them to become waterlogged, because they'll snuff out the coals. Instead, you want

Soak wood chips in water.

The charcoal is ready when it is white around the edges and holding a flame.

the wood chips to be wet on the outside, but not soaked through. The soaked chips should smolder some but also have the ability to hold a little fire and help heat the grill. As a general rule, soak wood chips for three to five minutes and baseball-size chunks for about fifteen minutes.

Before you add the soaked wood, you'll need to get the coals going. Some people don't use lighter fluid at all, because they don't like the idea of cooking over a petroleum product, but I like to use *a small amount* (a quick squirt) to get my fire going. If you saturate the coals it will produce a bad flavor in the meat. You can also use a chimney starter. Place some crumpled newspaper (or a few paraffin starters) in the bottom and fill with coal, then light the paper or starter with a match. When the coals are ready, lift the chimney.

Stack the coals in a pyramid on one side of the grill.

Spread the soaked chips over the white-hot coals for a dense smoke.

At this point, sometimes I leave the coals stacked in a pile, and sometimes I spread them out in an even layer. This decision depends on the size of the grill, the distance from the charcoal to the meat, and how I want my meat cooked. If I have a pit large enough, I'll heat up the charcoal in a pyramid on one side of the grill, and then, once the coals are hot, I'll spread them out and add the wood chips on top. If I have a smaller grill, I'll make a pyramid of charcoal in the center and place the meat around the edges of the grates. Sometimes at the end of the cooking process I'll place the meat directly over the charcoal to give it that heat blast to finish the cooking—I'm a well-done kinda guy.

The coals are ready for the wood when they are white around edges (they might also hold a little flame in the center). Spread the chips out over the coals, but don't bury them. Adding one layer to the hot coals will produce dynamite smoke. Gradually add more charcoal, as needed, to maintain your temperature.

CHARCOAL BRIQUETTES

Back in the day, charcoal was high maintenance—it was hard to light and would never stay lit. These days you can buy charwood (lump charcoal), natural briquettes, or composition briquettes (made from burned wood, coal dust, and paraffin binders) that are easy to light and reliable. A new variety that really turns me on is a combination of charcoal and hickory.

INTERNAL COOKING TEMPERATURES

A seasoned grill master can usually tell the doneness of a chicken breast or a steak by touching it, but the only surefire way to test the doneness of larger cuts of meat, like a pork shoulder or a Boston butt, is by using an instant-read meat thermometer. You should insert the thermometer into the thickest part of the cut, but don't allow the thermometer to touch the bone (bones conduct heat). You'll find visual guides to doneness in our recipes, but here is a general temperature guide.

Beef and Lamb (steak, roasts, chops)	
Rare	145°F
Medium-rare	150°F
Medium	160°F
Well-done	170°F
Ground Beef and Lamb	
Medium	160°F
Pork	
Medium	160°F
Well-done	170°F–190°F
Chicken and Turkey	
Medium	165°F

THE GOSPEL ACCORDING TO TONY

All these years over a pit have taught me a thing or two about perfect grilling. Here is a sampling of my secrets that will assure you of great results every time. And because I'm obsessive about these things (grilled meats, that is), I'll be back at you with even more tips in the barbecue section of the "Dig In: Savory, Soulful Entrées" chapter. Think of me as the great big barbecue angel (or brother) on your shoulder.

START FRESH: When it comes to meats, we start with fresh (not frozen). Frozen meats lose too much juice (and flavor) when they thaw, and can dry out on the grill.

GO LOW AND SLOW: Whether we're cooking at the restaurants or in the backyard, the Neely brothers always go *low and slow,* cooking away from the fire, using indirect heat. This method takes away the burn factor, because you won't have flare-ups, and it helps keep meat moist. Because we cook gently at a low temperature, we stay away from fattier cuts of meat: We don't need the fat to keep the meat moist; the cooking process does that. (By contrast, when you are grilling a big fat steak directly over a hot fire, you *need* that marbling so the meat doesn't burn and dry out.)

SEASON MEATS IN ADVANCE: When it comes to seasoning meats, the earlier the better. I prefer to season a pork shoulder or a slab of ribs the night before, then grill them off in the morning, to reheat later that night (or I season the meat in the morning and cook it off that night). But life doesn't always work that way, and if I don't get it done it isn't a deal breaker. Meat seasoned even an hour before grilling will taste more flavorful than if the seasoning is sprinkled on just before you cook.

SKIN-ON, BONE-IN IS ALWAYS BEST: Chicken and turkey skin and shrimp shells are juice retainers, which means more flavor in every bite. Bones hold cuts together and impart tremendous flavor during the cooking process.

GRILL RIBS CURL-SIDE UP: When it comes to ribs, the most important thing is retaining as much of the meat's natural juices as possible. For that reason, we cook the slabs curl-side up. This allows the juices to gather in the center of the curl (the meat practically bastes itself). I only flip once, halfway (or even three-quarters of the way) through the cooking process. You see these guys out there turning and turning the meat, but that just drains the meat of its juices, and there are always better things to do with your hands, no?

TONY'S GUIDE FOR BUYING MEATS

RIBS: A slab generally serves two or two and a half adults.

BARBECUED MEAT (PULLED PORK, TURKEY, BRISKET, ETC.): Four to five ounces of *finished* meat per person. Note that fattier meats lose a lot of yield during the cooking process. For instance, if you begin with six pounds of pork shoulder, you'll end up with about four and a half pounds, so plan accordingly. You'll have much less loss in yield from leaner meats like turkey and chicken. For instance, a three-pound boneless turkey breast will lose only about a quarter-pound during the cooking process.

Gimme a slab *this* big.

BARBECUED CHICKEN: One three- to four-pound bird generally feeds four people.

CATFISH: When it comes to catfish, you never think you'll have enough, and then you have too much—at least, that's how it goes at my house. I think this has something to do with how insubstantial the raw fish appear. I generally buy one fillet per person, or two fillets for a big eater (like me).

SHRIMP: Plan on about four ounces (or four or five extra jumbo shrimp) per person.

Note: I count kids under eleven as "half" adults, in terms of portion size.

Get the Party Started Neely-Style

Gina: Pat and I have a little routine that goes something like this. First I ask him to bring home some food from the restaurant because I'm thinking of having a few people over. Then one thing leads to another, and by the time he gets home, our driveway is packed with cars and the living room is jamming with family and friends. Of course, Pat teases me about my habit of turning "a few people" into a crowd, but he wouldn't have it any other way. After all, we are both happiest when our home is full of the people and the foods we love best. Plus, I get to be the queen bee for a night, and what's more fun than that?

I love preparing for my "house parties." I always light candles and load my CD player with five different sounds to set the mood. I also hire a bartender to assist guests who need help *getting* their mood together.

It's a recipe that has stood us well. Everyone eats, drinks, and has a good time, and when the music gets going, everyone beelines to the dance floor, where we relive our younger days. I'm the first one to step out (the queen bee is *always* the first one to step out), and then Pat falls in behind me, right in step. My husband is an undercover party man (he just doesn't know it).

We're all about fun down here in Memphis, so if you're thinking of showing up at one of our parties, check your baggage at the door!

When it comes to the cooking, we keep it simple and we keep it real. After we've put in such long days at the restaurant (and, these days, the television studio), the last thing we want to do is find ourselves working on our night off. That means serving **food that's simple, stylish, and not too fussy** but still packed with the bold flavors we love.

The following appetizers are meant to kick off a special dinner, create an amazing buffet of finger foods, or make incredible meals on their own. Of course, we can't

resist splashing some barbecue sauce into a few time-honored appetizers, and in this chapter you'll love the sweet tang our sauce brings to Barbecue Deviled Eggs and the sublime outrageousness Barbecue Pico de Gallo gives our Chicken Nachos with Green Chile Queso.

So now you have all our Neely secrets. What are you waiting for? Time to roll up your sleeves and fire up the blender. That's my idea of a party, for a crowd or just for my man and me. 🐖

Caribbean Rum Nuts

Gina: Girl, my favorite nut is the pecan! It is the all-American nut, and once you mix in cashews, you've got somethin' rocking. I serve this dangerously addictive appetizer at my "Girl Power" get-togethers because it's great with drinks (and because we ladies deserve a special treat).

The combination of dark rum and soy sauce gives these nuts their exotic flavor. For a true island feel, and a little kick, use a hot sauce made from Scotch bonnet peppers.

4 tablespoons butter
4 ounces (about 1 cup) pecan halves
4 ounces (about 1 cup) cashews
1/4 cup dark rum
1 tablespoon plus 1 teaspoon soy
    sauce
2 or 3 dashes hot sauce
Dash Worcestershire sauce
1 teaspoon kosher salt

Melt the butter in a large skillet over medium heat. Add the pecans and cashews, and cook, stirring, until the nuts have lightly browned, 5 to 6 minutes. Pour the rum over the nuts, and simmer until slightly reduced, about 1 minute. Add the soy sauce, hot sauce, Worcestershire sauce, and salt, and stir well to combine. Transfer the nuts to a plate covered with paper towels, and cool to room temperature.

MAKES ABOUT 2 CUPS (THEY WON'T LAST!)

NOTE: The nuts may soften slightly when heated, but they will regain their crispy texture when they cool.

Barbecue Deviled Eggs

Pat: When we were growing up, deviled eggs were a staple at any celebration, like a Fourth of July picnic or Easter Sunday brunch, and at family feasts at Momma's, alongside fried chicken, pork roast, green beans, and creamed corn. In my mind, deviled eggs are an appetizer or a snack, something you grab when you're passing through the kitchen or hanging out by the picnic table. But every once in a while, Momma served deviled eggs with tuna fish and crackers for a light Sunday dinner, proving that they can work as a meal just fine.

This is our spin on a great Southern tradition (one of the many joys of cooking is infusing a recipe with your own personality). The sweet, tangy flavor of barbecue sauce blends surprisingly well with rich, creamy egg yolks. Topped with thinly sliced scallions, these eggs are perfect for a picnic, a backyard party, a down-home brunch buffet, or a light Sunday dinner (thanks, Momma).

Gina: I wonder what the grandmothers would say about our adding barbecue sauce?

---

1 dozen large eggs
3 tablespoons mayonnaise
2 tablespoons Neely's Barbecue Sauce (page 25)
1 tablespoon plus 1 teaspoon prepared yellow mustard
Generous pinch kosher salt
Freshly ground black pepper
Dash or two hot sauce
2 scallions, very thinly sliced
Paprika, for garnish

Bring a medium saucepan of water to a lively simmer. Using a slotted spoon, gently lower the eggs into the water and simmer for 9 minutes. Reduce the heat if the simmer becomes too lively (so the eggs don't crack). Drain the water from the saucepan, and run cold water over the eggs until they are cool enough to handle. Peel the eggs, and cut them in half. Carefully remove the yolks (they should be slightly creamy) and place them in a small bowl. Add the mayonnaise, Neely's Barbecue Sauce, mustard, salt, pepper, and hot sauce, and whisk until the mixture is smooth. Use a small spoon to scoop the yolk mixture back into the whites (if you want to get fancy, you can use a pastry bag to pipe the yolks back into their whites). Garnish the tops with thinly sliced scallions and a dash of paprika.

MAKES 24 IRRESISTIBLE EGGS, SERVING 6 TO 8

NOTE: Deviled eggs are one exception to the "fresh is best" rule. When you boil fresh eggs, the whites have a tendency to cling to the shell. This complicates a simple task, but there's an easy way around it: let your eggs sit in the fridge for a week before you put them in the pot to boil. This will make peeling a snap.

Warm Artichoke and Collard Greens Dip

Gina: My friends call me the collard-green queen—I love to cook them up any and every way imaginable. So it was only a matter of time before I decided to replace spinach with collards in the classic artichoke dip. *Ohmigoodness,* the results were even better than I anticipated. If you want to surprise your friends with something delicious and unexpected, this is the appetizer to prepare.

You can buy baked pita chips to serve with this dip, but they're so fun and easy to make that you might just want to do it yourself (which also gives you a little more control over the amount of salt and oil used). This dip goes well with salsa and sour cream on the side.

---

4 tablespoons butter, plus more for
    greasing
1 cup finely chopped onion
2 garlic cloves, minced
¼ cup all-purpose flour
1 cup whole milk
1 cup heavy cream
⅔ cup grated Parmesan cheese
½ teaspoon salt
¼ teaspoon black pepper
Juice of ½ lemon
¼ teaspoon cayenne pepper
Dash Worcestershire sauce
Two 10-ounce boxes frozen collard
    greens, thawed and drained
One 12-ounce jar or can artichoke
    hearts, drained and coarsely
    chopped
½ cup shredded sharp cheddar
    cheese

Preheat the oven to 400°F. Lightly grease a 9-inch round chafing dish.

Melt the butter in a 2-quart saucepan over medium heat. Add the onion and garlic, and sauté until tender, about 3 minutes. Stir in the flour, and cook for 1 minute, until it reaches a golden-blond color.

Slowly whisk in the milk and cream, and bring to a low simmer. Add the Parmesan, and stir until the cheese has melted. Add the salt, black pepper, lemon juice, cayenne, and Worcestershire sauce. Fold in the collard greens and artichoke hearts. Transfer the mixture to a casserole dish, and top with the shredded cheddar cheese. Bake for 15 to 20 minutes, or until golden brown.

SERVES 6 TO 8

Pita Chips

Three 8- to 10-inch pita rounds
1 large garlic clove, smashed and
   halved
4 tablespoons olive oil
½ teaspoon kosher salt
½ teaspoon dried oregano
2 tablespoons grated Parmesan
   cheese

Preheat the oven to 375°F.

Rub each pita round with the smashed garlic, and then brush with olive oil. Cut each round into eight wedges and arrange on a baking sheet. Sprinkle the wedges with salt, oregano, and Parmesan, and bake for 8 to 10 minutes, until lightly golden.

Creamy Herb Dip

Gina: We serve plenty of meals that are heavy on the pork fat—and we wouldn't have it any other way! That's why I like to balance out some menus with fresh vegetables and this classic creamy herb dip. It's also a great way to get my girls and (big Neely) boys to eat their veggies.

I like to serve this dip with vegetable crudités: try red and orange cherry tomatoes, blanched asparagus spears and broccoli florets, fresh radishes, green onions, and carrots. It also makes a fabulous spread for turkey or ham sandwiches.

8 ounces reduced-fat cream cheese, softened
½ cup sour cream
½ cup mayonnaise
4 scallions, white and green parts, finely chopped
2 tablespoons finely chopped fresh flat-leaf parsley
1 tablespoon finely chopped fresh dill
1 teaspoon kosher salt
¾ teaspoon freshly ground black pepper
½ teaspoon Old Bay Seasoning
¼ teaspoon cayenne pepper

Place all the ingredients in the bowl of an electric mixer fitted with the paddle attachment and blend until smooth. Chill for at least 1 hour before serving.

MAKES 2 CUPS

Pimento Cheese Melts (aka Southern Crostini)

Gina: A few years ago, Pat and I had the honor of visiting Madrid, Spain, to cook at the U.S. Consulate there. The idea was for the Spaniards to taste some real Southern barbecue (see page 52). Well, my poor husband got straight off a plane and headed for a makeshift smoker, while I got to lounge in a fabulous hotel and drink champagne. But the dinner turned out to be a huge hit, and afterward we got to celebrate by exploring the city and hitting several tapas bars. When I saw that the streets and the restaurants were still buzzing with folks of all ages late into the evening, I decided the Spanish have it down—they know how to have a good time.

When Pat and I got home, we decided to put our own spin on a favorite tapas dish. Down South, we like our "crostini," or grilled toasts, with a little soul. So we started with a rich, creamy pimento cheese that we love and gave it a little kick with the addition of some cayenne pepper. For a truly Southern spin, we added crumbled bacon (Pat and I will find a way to incorporate pork into just about any recipe).

As a finish, we slathered the cheese spread on toasted bread and sprinkled the crumbled bacon on top, then slipped the toasts under the broiler until the cheese was just melted. Good Lord, what's not to love?

These toasts are amazing with chilled white wine. Covered and chilled, the pimento-cheese spread will last for up to 3 days in the refrigerator.

---

4 strips bacon
8 ounces extra-sharp white
    cheddar, grated
8 ounces extra-sharp orange
    cheddar, grated
One 7-ounce jar pimentos, drained
    and finely chopped
½ teaspoon black pepper
½ teaspoon garlic powder
¼ teaspoon cayenne pepper, or
    more to taste
¾ cup mayonnaise
1 baguette

Cook the bacon until crisp, and then transfer it to a plate lined with paper towels to cool.

Combine the white and orange cheddar, pimentos, black pepper, garlic powder, cayenne, and mayonnaise in the bowl of an electric mixer fitted with the paddle attachment. Stir at low speed until well blended (there will be flecks of pimento throughout). Chill for at least 2 hours to allow the flavors to develop.

Preheat the oven to 400°F.

Cut the baguette into ½-inch-thick slices. Toast them in the oven for 2 to 3 minutes on each side, until golden. Spread a generous amount of the pimento spread on each toast, and top with a crumbling of bacon. Return to the oven and bake until the cheese is melted, about 2 more minutes.

MAKES ABOUT 3 CUPS OF PIMENTO CHEESE, ENOUGH FOR SEVERAL BAGUETTES

From Memphis to Madrid

Pat: **"MEMPHIS IN MAY"** is one of the most spectacular events in the state of Tennessee. Every year for the event, which consists of a giant music festival and a "World Championship Barbecue Cooking Contest," Memphis honors a country, and we invite delegates from that country to our city for some down-home Southern hospitality.

In 2007, we honored Spain. Traditionally, we send the Memphis in May board, along with local political and business leaders, on an advance visit to the country we are honoring. That year, the U.S. ambassador to Spain was a Texan, and when he found out Memphis was coming his way, he asked if we could bring some barbecue (he was obviously homesick for some good barbecue). Who can blame him? Kevin Kane, the president of the Memphis Convention and Visitors Bureau, asked if I would supply the barbecue for an event in Madrid. A few months before, I'd been voted Restaurateur of the Year by the Memphis Restaurant Association, and was ridin' high and feelin' like I could do *anything*. So I agreed. I figured I could prep everything in my restaurants and ship it over. Since it was for the U.S. ambassador, I didn't anticipate any U.S. Customs problems.

So much for my best-laid plans. As we prepared to go to Spain, I found out that the only things I could ship were my sauce and seasoning. Boy oh boy, was I in trouble. I needed to come up with a solution—fast. I started researching barbecue places in Madrid, and finally found Alfredo's Barbacoa, owned by a New Yorker. I gave him a call, and he was gracious enough to let me cook in his restaurant, under two conditions: We get him and his family tickets to the big party, and I do my prep work when the restaurant closed at midnight.

Gina and I arrived in Spain around 5:00 p.m. (remember, there's a seven-hour time difference, and with the connections it took us fifteen hours to get there). When we arrived, I beat it to the restaurant with Kevin and Chris Roan (another MCVB executive), who promised to help out with this crazy endeavor. I don't think my colleagues realized the night we were in for—we needed to prepare ribs, chicken, barbecue spaghetti, and coleslaw for two hundred people and wrap up around dawn the next day. Needless to say, when I got back to the hotel, I had been up for more than thirty-six hours and was butt-ass tired.

Even though Barbacoa didn't have a traditional barbecue pit—theirs was a flat-top about four feet long—the food turned out great. The night of the event, all I saw were smiles of contentment, and the Memphians who flew over seemed very proud that our great barbecue tradition had traveled so far and so well. 🐖

From fishing and horseback riding to just hanging out with my siblings, our home was always full of excitement.

TOP ROW: Mark Neely in a tux; (from left to right) Gaelin, Pat, Mark, and Tony in the front yard.

Homemade Cheddar and Pecan Crisps

Gina: These crispy crackers—cheese, nuts, and a serious visit from the spice fairy—are my kind of snack. I like this recipe because it makes several logs of dough, giving me a few to bake off now and a few more to have in the freezer, for the next time guests stop by. These crisps are the perfect holiday appetizer, when folks are overloaded on sweets and craving a savory snack to have with their drinks.

1 pound extra-sharp cheddar, grated
1 cup plus 1 tablespoon butter
1⅓ cups pecans
Kosher salt
2 cups all-purpose flour
1¼ teaspoons cayenne pepper
½ teaspoon black pepper

Preheat the oven to 350°F.

Coarsely grate the cheddar cheese, and transfer it to the bowl of an electric mixer fitted with the paddle attachment. Cut the two sticks of butter into sixteen pieces, and scatter the pieces over the cheese. Let the cheese and butter soften. Place the pecans in one layer on a baking sheet, and toast them in the oven until they are a shade darker and fragrant, 7 to 8 minutes. While the nuts are still warm, transfer them to a medium bowl and toss with the remaining tablespoon of butter (the hot nuts will melt the butter) and salt to taste. Cool the nuts completely, then finely chop.

Add the chopped pecans, flour, a pinch of salt, cayenne, and black pepper to the bowl of the mixer, and beat the ingredients at medium speed until the mixture pulls together into a dough, about 2 minutes.

Divide the dough into eight pieces. On a sheet of waxed paper, roll each piece of the dough into a log 1 inch in diameter, and wrap the logs tightly in waxed paper and foil. Chill the logs for at least 8 hours and up to 1 week. The dough will keep frozen for 2 months.

Preheat the oven to 350°F.

Working with one log at a time, cut the log crosswise into ⅛-inch-thick slices, and arrange the slices ½ inch apart on parchment-lined baking sheets. Bake the crisps in batches until they are golden and just firm to the touch, 10 to 12 minutes. Cool the wafers on the baking sheet. Stored in an airtight container at room temperature, the wafers will keep for up to 4 days.

MAKES ABOUT 100 CRISPS

Chicken Nachos with Green Chile Queso and Barbecue Pico

Gina: This appetizer—a Neely Señoritas' Night favorite—couldn't be easier to prepare (or more satisfying to eat). I use the meat from a store-bought roasted chicken, and combine it with tortilla chips and a homemade version of that molten guilty pleasure, cheese dip made from processed cheese (*hola,* Velveeta!). I also add Southwestern flavors, like green onions, pickled jalapeños, and cilantro, and a Neely finish, Barbecue Pico de Gallo, which gets its sweet, tangy undertone from our sauce (and comes together in minutes in the food processor).

Chicken nachos are a great appetizer, especially when there's a game on television, but they also make a fun end-of-week dinner with a couple of cold beers. So, whether the occasion is Señoritas' Night (put on the salsa music, girl) or game day, these nachos are always a hit.

---

1 roasted or barbecued chicken
Kosher salt
Freshly ground black pepper

GREEN-CHILE QUESO
2 tablespoons butter
1 small onion, minced
1 small red bell pepper, finely
    chopped
1 or 2 serrano chiles, seeded and
    finely chopped
1 garlic clove, minced
2 medium tomatoes, diced (or one
    14.5-ounce can diced tomatoes,
    drained)
One 4-ounce can chopped green
    chiles (see note)
1 pound processed American cheese
    (such as Velveeta), cubed

NACHOS
One 16-ounce bag tortilla chips
1 bunch scallions, thinly sliced
½ cup sliced pickled jalapeños
2 tablespoons chopped fresh
    cilantro leaves, for garnish
1 cup Barbecue Pico de Gallo (recipe
    follows), for serving

Using your hands, pull the meat from the chicken, discarding the skin and bones. Use a fork to shred the meat. Transfer the chicken meat to a mixing bowl, season with salt and pepper, and toss to combine.

Melt the butter in a large skillet over medium-low heat. When the butter starts to sizzle, add the onion, bell pepper, serrano chiles, and garlic, and cook, stirring, for 3 to 4 minutes, until the vegetables are tender. Add the tomatoes and chopped green chiles, and cook for 2 more minutes. Add the cubed cheese, and stir until melted; cover to keep warm.

Preheat the oven to 400°F.

Spread the tortilla chips on a baking sheet or in a large, shallow casserole dish. Top the chips with the chicken, the warm queso, and then the scallions and jalapeños. Bake until the cheese is melted and bubbly and the nachos are heated through, 8 to 10 minutes. Garnish with cilantro, and serve with the Barbecue Pico de Gallo on the side.

SERVES 6

NOTE: Look for canned green chiles that are "fire-roasted," as they have the most flavor.

Barbecue Pico de Gallo

One 14.5-ounce can diced tomatoes,
   with juice
½ cup Neely's Barbecue Sauce
   (page 25)
¼ cup chopped yellow onion
⅓ cup chopped fresh cilantro leaves
2 teaspoons fresh lime juice
1 garlic clove, minced
1 tablespoon hot sauce
¼ teaspoon salt

Combine all the ingredients in the bowl of a food processor, and pulse until the salsa is of uniform consistency but still slightly chunky. Transfer to a serving bowl.

MAKES 2 GENEROUS CUPS

Gina and Food Network
stylist Brianna Blagg
having fun in the kitchen

Pat's Wings of Fire with Horseradish Dipping Sauce

Gina: They call me the spice fairy on our show, but my husband is the *hot man*! If you can't take the heat, you might want to reconsider this dish.

Pat: Living in the South, I have, of course, acquired a taste for both spicy food and fried chicken. In fact, I love fried chicken so much that I eat it at least once a week. And the wings happen to be my favorite part of the bird. No cut is more succulent or flavorful, especially when dusted with fiery seasonings, dipped in batter, and fried.

To fire up the flavor in this recipe, I season both the wings and the batter with cayenne, red-pepper flakes, black pepper, and even a little hot sauce. Like Gina says, I just can't seem to get enough spice or fire.

I should add that Gina not only understands my fried-chicken affliction, she encourages it, and several years ago, she went so far as to purchase me a countertop fryer. This has made it easy for me to come home any night and fry up some chicken (it has also saved on time and mess). You will definitely want to adjust the heat levels in this recipe. I have to do the same thing at home, because if it's too hot my girls won't eat it.

SPICY CHICKEN SEASONING

1 tablespoon Neely's Barbecue
   Seasoning (page 22)
1 tablespoon crushed red-pepper
   flakes
2 teaspoons black pepper
2 teaspoons cayenne pepper
2 teaspoons poultry seasoning
1 teaspoon lemon pepper
12 whole chicken wings, cut apart at
   the joint

SPICY CHICKEN BATTER

3 eggs
2 tablespoons hot sauce
1 tablespoon crushed red-pepper
   flakes
1 teaspoon black pepper
1 teaspoon cayenne pepper
2 cups all-purpose flour
Vegetable or peanut oil, for
   deep-frying

In a small bowl, whisk together the Neely's Barbecue Seasoning, red-pepper flakes, black pepper, cayenne, poultry seasoning, and lemon pepper. Reserve 2 tablespoons of this mixture in a separate bowl.

Rinse the chicken wings in cold water, and then place them in a shallow baking dish and pat them dry with paper towels. Sprinkle the wings evenly with the Spicy Chicken Seasoning, cover the dish with plastic wrap, and chill for 1 hour.

Whisk the eggs, hot sauce, red-pepper flakes, black pepper, and cayenne together in a medium mixing bowl. Place the flour in a shallow pie plate.

Heat the oil in a deep fryer or a Dutch oven (1½ inches deep) over medium-high heat until it reaches 350°F on a deep-fat thermometer.

Dip the chicken wings in the egg mixture, shaking off the excess, then in the flour. This process will be neater if you can keep one hand dry. Place half the wings in the hot oil and fry for 8 to 10 minutes, turning occasionally, until they are cooked through and golden brown. Use tongs to transfer the wings to a paper towel–lined tray. Allow the oil to return to cooking temperature before adding the next batch. For extra hot results, sprinkle the cooked wings with the reserved seasoning. Serve with Horseradish Dipping Sauce (recipe follows).

SERVES 2 OR 3

Horseradish Dipping Sauce

1 cup mayonnaise

2 scallions, green and white parts, finely chopped

2 tablespoons prepared (or grated fresh) horseradish

¼ cup chili sauce (such as Heinz)

¼ teaspoon cayenne pepper

Mix all the ingredients together in a small bowl, and refrigerate until needed.

Florida Coast Pickled Shrimp

Gina: We've taken a few memorable family vacations to the Gulf Coast of Florida, which is a great place to indulge our passion for the beach—and fresh shrimp. These pickled shrimp are perfect for entertaining, because they are actually best made a day in advance. They're delicious on their own, or eaten with buttered slices of French bread.

One 3-ounce bag crab-boil spices (such as Zatarain's)
4 teaspoons kosher salt
2 lemons, quartered
2 pounds medium shrimp, shelled and deveined if you wish
2 cups vegetable oil
1 cup red-wine vinegar
½ cup fresh lime juice
2 tablespoons Creole mustard (see page 93)
2 teaspoons black peppercorns
2 teaspoons fennel seeds
1 teaspoon crushed red-pepper flakes
4 garlic cloves, peeled and crushed
4 bay leaves
2 large sweet onions, thinly sliced
2 large carrots, thinly sliced
2 lemons, thinly sliced

In a large pot, combine the crab boil, 2 teaspoons of the salt, the lemon quarters, and 8 cups water. Bring the mixture to a boil, and boil for 5 minutes. Add the shrimp, and cook until they are pink and cooked through, about 3 minutes. Drain the shrimp in a colander, and discard the crab boil and lemon.

In a small saucepan, whisk together the oil, vinegar, lime juice, Creole mustard, peppercorns, fennel seeds, red-pepper flakes, garlic, bay leaves, and the remaining 2 teaspoons salt. Bring to a boil, then reduce the heat and simmer for 2 minutes. Remove the pan from the heat, stir in the onions and carrots, and cool completely. Place the shrimp in a large nonreactive mixing bowl or container (sealable plastic storage containers work great), and cover with the marinade. Toss with the lemon slices, cover tightly, and refrigerate for at least 8 hours (or for up to 2 days), tossing every 4 or so hours, before serving. To serve the pickled shrimp, use a slotted spoon to transfer the shrimp and goodies (pickled veggies, spices) to a serving bowl, then add just enough liquid to keep everything moist (using the entire bowl of pickling liquid would be too messy).

SERVES 6 TO 8

NOTE: We call for the shrimp to be shelled and deveined in this recipe, because it allows the shrimp to really soak up the marinade. But if you are pressed for time, and your friends don't mind getting their nails dirty, leave the shells on. The shrimp are just as good, and the extra effort your friends have to exert to extract the shrimp from their shells may produce an unexpected benefit: leftovers!

Crab Cakes with Lime Mayonnaise

Gina: Pat is a meat-and-potatoes man, but me, I've gotta have my crab cakes. Every year, we go to a fancy restaurant in Memphis for our wedding anniversary, and I order crab cakes off the menu every time. I love them so much that Pat has started making them at home. Do you think he's being cheap or treating me special? The secret to these crab cakes is using plenty of crab and not too much filling. The sunny Lime Mayonnaise packs a piquant punch.

2 tablespoons butter, melted and cooled

¼ cup mayonnaise

1 egg, lightly beaten

3 scallions, green and white parts, finely chopped

1 garlic clove, minced

2 tablespoons chopped fresh flat-leaf parsley leaves

2 tablespoons fresh lemon juice

2 teaspoons Creole mustard (see page 93)

1 teaspoon Worcestershire sauce

1 teaspoon paprika

1 teaspoon salt

Dash cayenne pepper

2 or 3 grindings fresh black pepper

1 pound lump crabmeat, picked free of shells

1 cup soft fresh bread crumbs (see note)

¼ cup cornmeal

½ cup peanut oil

1 recipe Lime Mayonnaise (recipe follows), for serving

In a large bowl, whisk together the butter, mayonnaise, egg, scallions, garlic, parsley, lemon juice, Creole mustard, Worcestershire sauce, paprika, salt, cayenne, and black pepper. Gently fold in the crabmeat and bread crumbs until they are just combined. Press the crab mixture into ½-cup measures, gently shape into six patties, then transfer the cakes to a baking sheet lined with parchment paper and dusted with half of the cornmeal. Sprinkle the tops of the cakes with the remaining cornmeal; cover and chill for at least 30 minutes, or up to 2 hours.

Preheat the oven to 200°F.

Heat the oil in a large skillet over medium heat. When the oil is hot, carefully place crab cakes, in batches, in the pan, and fry the cakes until golden brown and crisp, 4 to 5 minutes. Carefully flip the crab cakes, and fry on the other side until golden brown, about 4 minutes. Keep the cakes warm on a baking sheet in the oven while you fry the remaining cakes. Serve them warm with Lime Mayonnaise.

MAKES 6 CRAB CAKES

NOTE: Soft, fresh bread crumbs help crab cakes bind together better than dry bread crumbs, and they yield a lighter, more tender final result. A firm, white sandwich bread like Pepperidge Farm, trimmed of crusts and ground in a food processor, is a great choice (you can also use a baguette).

Lime Mayonnaise

1 cup mayonnaise
1 large shallot, minced
Zest of 1 lime
2 tablespoons fresh lime juice
1 serrano chile, seeded and minced
2 tablespoons chopped fresh
    cilantro leaves

Stir together all the ingredients in a small mixing bowl, and chill until needed.

MAKES A GENEROUS CUP

Grilled Gorgonzola Toasts with Sweet Peppers

Pat: When the grill is fired up for dinner—as it often is in our house—these toasts make great appetizers. The grilled vegetables and vinegar create an appealing relish that's the perfect foil for Gorgonzola cheese. The pungent, savory flavors are a fantastic kickoff to a juicy grilled steak and a killer bottle of red wine.

2 garlic cloves, peeled

⅓ cup olive oil

1 large baguette

1 red bell pepper, seeded and sliced into thin strips

1 yellow bell pepper, seeded and sliced into thin strips

4 plum tomatoes, halved and grilled

3 tablespoons julienned fresh basil leaves

2 tablespoons balsamic vinegar

1 tablespoon capers, drained

Kosher salt

Freshly ground black pepper

4 ounces creamy Gorgonzola or other blue cheese, at room temperature

Preheat a grill to 375°F (or turn on the broiler).

Place the garlic cloves and olive oil in a saucepan, and heat gently for 1 to 2 minutes, to flavor the oil (be careful not to burn the garlic or it will turn acrid and bitter). Discard the garlic.

Cut the baguette into ½-inch-thick slices, brush the slices lightly with the garlic oil (you will have some left over) and grill them (or toast them) until crisp, 1 to 2 minutes. Set the bread aside, uncovered, so that it will remain crisp while you prepare the vegetables.

Slice the bell peppers lengthwise into ½-inch-thick slices. Brush the bell peppers and tomato halves with the remaining garlic oil, and grill or broil on both sides until lightly charred but still firm. Cool the vegetables for several minutes before roughly chopping and tossing them in a bowl with the basil, vinegar, capers, salt and pepper to taste, and any remaining oil.

Slather the toasts with the softened Gorgonzola, and top each one with a spoonful of the grilled pepper-and-tomato mixture and a grinding of black pepper.

SERVES 6 TO 8

CLOCKWISE FROM ABOVE: Gina's fifth grade photo; Gina in front of the Mound Community Center; Gina at a high school pep rally before a big game; Gina and Tony with colleagues at a holiday party; Gina at SeaWorld in San Diego; Gina with her niece Kandyce and big sister Kim on Kandyce's first birthday

Grilled Shrimp, Scallion, and Bacon Quesadillas with Smoky Guacamole

Gina: Just a few minutes on a hot grill will give shrimp and scallions a wonderful charred, smoky flavor, making an incredible filling for crisp and gooey quesadillas. The smoky flavor is echoed in the guacamole, which is made with chipotle peppers in adobo.

2 tablespoons olive oil, plus more for frying tortillas
4 strips thick-sliced bacon, cut into ½-inch pieces
12 large shrimp, peeled and deveined
1 garlic clove, minced
Kosher salt
Freshly ground black pepper
3 scallions
Four 12-inch flour tortillas
8 ounces (about 2 cups) shredded Jack cheese
1 recipe Smoky Guacamole (recipe follows), for serving

Heat 1 tablespoon of the olive oil in a medium skillet over medium heat. When the oil is hot, add the bacon and fry until crisp. Transfer the bacon to a plate lined with paper towels.

Heat the grill (or a grill pan) to a medium-high setting. Place the shrimp, garlic, remaining tablespoon of oil, and salt and pepper in a medium bowl, and toss to combine. When the grill is hot, use tongs to place the shrimp and scallions across the grates. Cook until the shrimp are pink and firm (2 to 3 minutes on each side), and the scallions are charred and softened (turning them as necessary for even cooking). Transfer the shrimp and scallions to a plate to cool briefly, then coarsely chop both ingredients, toss them together in a clean bowl, and cover to keep warm.

Preheat the oven to 200°F.

Wipe out the skillet with a paper towel, return it to the heat, and add another drizzle of oil and a tortilla. Cook the tortilla for 30 seconds, then flip it. Cover half of the tortilla with a couple of spoonfuls of cheese. Arrange a quarter of the shrimp-and-garlic mixture and a quarter of the bacon over the cheese, and fold the tortilla over. Press down gently with a spatula and cook the tortilla for a minute or so on each side, to melt cheese and crisp. Transfer the cooked quesadilla to a baking sheet and hold in the oven while you repeat the process with the remaining ingredients. Cut each quesadilla into five wedges, and transfer to plates with your spatula. Top the wedges with liberal amounts of Smoky Guacamole.

SERVES 4

Smoky Guacamole

2 large ripe avocados
½ medium onion, finely chopped
1 chipotle pepper in adobo sauce,
    finely chopped
2 tablespoons fresh lime juice
½ cup chopped fresh cilantro leaves
Kosher salt

Peel and pit the avocados, and place them in a medium bowl. Add the onion, chipotle pepper, lime juice, and cilantro, and mash together with a fork until combined but still chunky. Season to taste with salt.

MAKES ABOUT 1¼ CUPS

NOTES: If you don't feel like firing up the grill, you can simply sauté coarsely chopped shrimp (or diced chicken breasts, for that matter), scallions, and garlic in a little olive oil for 2 to 3 minutes, until the shrimp (or chicken) are cooked through.

Canned chipotle peppers in adobo are available in the Mexican section of most supermarkets.

Coconut Shrimp with Spicy Peanut Sauce

Gina: This appetizer is a signature dish at beach bars throughout Mexico (where Pat and I often retreat for some serious R & R) and the Caribbean. It tastes like a tropical vacation. Large, sweet shrimp are dipped in coconut, fried until crisp, and then paired with a sweet and spicy peanut sauce. Honey, pass the frozen blender drinks, because I am so there—dipping my feet in the sand.

24 large (31- to 35-count) shrimp, peeled, deveined, and butterflied (do not remove tail)
½ cup all-purpose flour
2 tablespoons cornstarch
1½ teaspoons Chinese five-spice powder
1 teaspoon kosher salt
¼ teaspoon freshly ground black pepper
¼ teaspoon cayenne pepper
1 cup beer (not dark)
1½ cups sweetened shredded coconut
1 cup Japanese panko bread crumbs
Canola or peanut oil, for frying
2 cups Spicy Peanut Sauce (recipe follows)

Pat the shrimp dry with a paper towel. In a medium bowl, whisk together the flour, cornstarch, five-spice powder, salt, black pepper, cayenne, and beer until smooth. In another bowl, combine the shredded coconut with the bread crumbs. Holding the shrimp by the tail, dip them into the batter, allowing any excess to drip off, and then dip them into the coconut bread crumbs (turning and pressing to get full coverage). Keeping one hand dry will make this whole process neater.

In a large pot or Dutch oven, heat 1 inch of oil to 365°F. Gently submerge shrimp, about six at a time, and fry for about 3 minutes, or until golden brown. Transfer the shrimp to a paper towel–lined plate and sprinkle lightly with additional salt. Serve the shrimp warm, with Spicy Peanut Sauce.

SERVES 4 TO 6

NOTES: Chinese five-spice powder has an alluring perfume and spicy-sweet flavor that can't be beat. The traditional spices are cinnamon, star anise, aniseed, ginger, and Sichuan peppercorns, although some blends also include cloves. It is available in the spice section of most supermarkets, or at Asian specialty-food stores.

Japanese panko bread crumbs are made from wheat bread, and they are lighter and crispier than regular bread crumbs.

Spicy Peanut Sauce

1 garlic clove, coarsely chopped

1 tablespoon chopped fresh ginger

¼ cup Chicken Stock (page 28)

½ cup unsweetened coconut milk

Zest of 1 lime

Juice of 1 lime

2 tablespoons soy sauce

1 tablespoon Asian fish sauce

1 to 2 tablespoons Sriracha
   (Vietnamese chile sauce),
   or to taste

¾ cup creamy peanut butter

½ cup chopped fresh cilantro
   (leaves and tender stems)

Place the garlic and ginger in a food processor and pulse until finely chopped. Add the stock, coconut milk, lime zest and juice, soy sauce, fish sauce, and sriracha, and purée. Add the peanut butter, and pulse to combine. Fold in the cilantro, and refrigerate until ready to serve.

Bring the sauce to room temperature, and serve it with the coconut shrimp.

MAKES ABOUT 2 CUPS

Southern Soups and Stews

Pat: One evening, I was in the kitchen—chopping onions, having a glass of wine, and preparing dinner—when my older daughter, Spenser, came walking through the door, humming to herself and smiling, content in her own little world. A few minutes later, our younger daughter, Shelbi, did the exact same thing. The simple beauty of the moment—preparing dinner for my family, and realizing that we had raised two happy, healthy girls who felt secure in the world—practically stopped me in my tracks. There is nothing more important to me than family, and nothing more wonderful than preparing a meal for them in our home.

Preparing and enjoying a simmering pot of soup or stew is the embodiment of that feeling, which is about being emotionally and physically *full.* So whenever I'm making soup, whether it's a recipe from childhood, like Nana's Southern Gumbo or my mother's Hearty Beef Stew, or the girls are turning me on to something new, like Vegetarian Chili, I always feel good. 🐷

Spicy Corn Chowder

Pat: This creamy corn chowder, packed with vegetables and spices, has more sass than your average chowder (and the sweet potato and spices give it a distinct orange hue). The ingredients—smoky bacon, fresh herbs, and a little Neely kick (cayenne pepper)—combine for an over-the-top, out-of-this-world chowder flavor. When corn is at its peak, during the summer, we use fresh kernels straight from the cob. But since we crave this soup all year long, we use frozen corn as well and get great results. If you use frozen corn, look for the white kernels—they are particularly sweet.

---

1 tablespoon olive oil

4 strips thick-sliced bacon, cut into ½-inch pieces

1 large onion, finely chopped (about 2 cups)

1 large carrot, finely chopped (1 cup)

1 celery stalk, finely chopped (¾ cup)

1 red bell pepper, finely chopped (1 cup)

2 tablespoons flour

½ pound yellow-fleshed potatoes such as Yukon Gold (2 small), peeled and cut into ¼-inch dice

½ pound dark-skinned sweet potato (1 medium), peeled and cut into ¼-inch dice

6 cups Chicken Stock (page 28)

1 tablespoon smoked paprika

1 teaspoon kosher salt

1 teaspoon black pepper

½ teaspoon cayenne pepper

4 cups corn kernels (from about 6 ears or two 10-ounce boxes frozen corn)

1 cup heavy cream

1 tablespoon chopped fresh thyme leaves (or 1 teaspoon dried thyme)

Heat the olive oil in a large, heavy pot over medium heat. When the oil is hot, add the bacon and cook, stirring frequently, until crisp, about 5 minutes. Using a slotted spoon, transfer the cooked bacon to paper towels to drain. Add the onion, carrot, celery, and bell pepper to the pot, and cook, stirring, until softened, about 3 minutes. Add the flour. Cook and stir for 3 more minutes.

Add the potatoes, broth, paprika, salt, black pepper, and cayenne. Simmer, covered, until the potatoes are tender, about 15 minutes. Add the corn and cream, and simmer, uncovered, for 30 minutes. Add the fresh thyme. Season to taste with additional salt and pepper, and serve garnished with the crisp bacon.

MAKES 8 SERVINGS

Silky Carrot Soup

Pat: When Gina and I are on a fitness kick and determined to lose a few pounds, I love having healthy, vibrant vegetable soups on hand. The soups help us fight the flab without sacrificing taste. And they fill us up, too! We often serve soup as a nourishing lunch or first course, and this carrot soup is one of my favorites. It has a velvety texture and an orange color that pops, and it includes a secret ingredient (sweet potato) and warm spices like cumin, coriander, and cayenne to give it depth and an irresistible aroma. Puréeing this soup in a blender instead of a food processor makes it especially silky. It's great hot, but it's also good chilled, topped with a swirl of plain yogurt or sour cream, during our sultry Memphis summers.

5 cups Chicken Stock (page 28)
1 pound carrots, coarsely chopped
2 medium celery stalks, coarsely
    chopped
1 large onion, coarsely chopped
1 leek, white and tender green parts
    only, coarsely chopped
1 small sweet potato (about
    6 ounces), peeled and
    coarsely chopped
2 teaspoons grated fresh ginger
1 1/2 teaspoons ground cumin
1 teaspoon ground coriander
1/4 teaspoon cayenne pepper
1 cup well-shaken buttermilk
2 tablespoons fresh lemon juice
Salt
Freshly ground black pepper
2 tablespoons coarsely chopped
    fresh flat-leaf parsley leaves

In a large pot, combine the stock with the carrots, celery, onion, leek, potato, ginger, cumin, coriander, and cayenne, and bring to a boil. Cover, and simmer over low heat until the vegetables are tender, 20 to 25 minutes.

Working in batches, purée the soup in a blender or a food processor, then return to the pot. Stir in the buttermilk and lemon juice, and season with salt and black pepper. Reheat gently. Ladle into bowls, sprinkle with the parsley, and serve.

SERVES 6 TO 8

Spicy Tomato Soup with Avocado Relish

Pat: This is our kind of tomato soup—it has plenty of attitude! A double dose of heat (crushed red-pepper flakes and chipotle-pepper purée) gives it a smoky undertone; a garnish of avocado relish balances the flavors and provides an appealing texture. This soup is delicious with hot cornbread or grilled ham-and-cheese sandwiches.

2 tablespoons olive oil

1 medium onion, finely chopped

2 celery stalks, finely chopped

2 carrots, peeled, finely chopped

3 garlic cloves, minced

2 teaspoons fresh thyme leaves, finely chopped

½ teaspoon dried crushed red-pepper flakes

Kosher salt

Two 28-ounce cans peeled plum tomatoes with juice

6 cups chicken broth

2 bay leaves

2 tablespoons chopped chipotle peppers in adobo sauce

1 to 2 teaspoons sherry-wine vinegar

Freshly ground black pepper

AVOCADO RELISH

1 large avocado, peeled, pitted, and diced

½ small red onion, finely chopped

½ seedless cucumber, peeled and chopped

⅓ cup chopped fresh cilantro leaves

1 serrano chile, seeded and finely chopped

2 tablespoons fresh lime juice

Kosher salt

Heat the olive oil in a large, heavy pot over medium heat. Add the onion, celery, carrots, garlic, thyme, red-pepper flakes, and a pinch of salt, and cook, stirring, until the ingredients are fragrant and tender, about 5 minutes. Add the tomatoes, broth, and bay leaves, and bring to a boil. Reduce the heat to low, and simmer for 30 minutes.

Meanwhile, make the avocado relish. Combine the avocado, red onion, cucumber, cilantro, serrano chile, lime juice, and a generous sprinkling of salt in a medium bowl. Taste for seasonings, and add more salt or lime as desired.

After the soup has simmered, discard the bay leaves and stir in the chipotle peppers and vinegar. Working in batches, purée the soup in a blender or a food processor and return it to the pot. Season the purée with additional salt and freshly ground black pepper to taste, and serve each portion garnished with a few tablespoons of the avocado relish.

SERVES 8

White Bean Soup with Kale

Pat: Creamy, smoky white beans, simmered with some kind of pork fat, are a Southern staple, especially when served with a wedge of warm cornbread. This white-bean soup is finished with kale, a nourishing green that's packed with vitamins A and C (the leaves are so pretty that Gina uses the green and purple varieties to decorate her party trays). Smoked sausage makes a great addition to this soup, and what we do then is leave out the bacon and add ½ pound of sliced smoked sausage instead. (You've heard the expression "an eye for an eye"—in Memphis we say "a pig for a pig.")

---

1 pound dried white beans, such as
    Great Northern, cannellini,
    or navy
3 tablespoons olive oil
1 large onion, chopped
2 leeks, white and pale-green parts
    only, sliced (about 1 cup)
1 large tomato, seeded and chopped
1 large carrot, chopped
2 celery stalks, chopped
8 garlic cloves, finely chopped
3 strips thick-sliced bacon, chopped
8 cups Chicken Stock (page 28)
1 tablespoon chopped fresh thyme
    leaves
1 teaspoon chopped fresh rosemary
    leaves
2 cups water
1 pound kale, stems and center ribs
    discarded, leaves coarsely
    chopped
Kosher salt
Freshly ground black pepper
Hot sauce

Place the beans in a large pot. Add enough water to cover by 2 inches, and soak the beans overnight. Drain.

Heat the olive oil in a large pot over medium-high heat. Add the onion, leeks, tomato, carrot, celery, garlic, and bacon, and sauté until the vegetables are tender, about 6 minutes. Add the beans, stock, thyme, rosemary, and water, and bring the soup to a boil. Reduce the heat to medium-low, then cover and simmer, stirring occasionally, until the beans are very tender, about 50 minutes. Then stir in the kale and simmer until the leaves are tender, about 15 more minutes. Season the soup to taste with salt, pepper, and hot sauce.

SERVES 6 TO 8

NOTE: Like most soups, this one is best if made 1 or 2 days ahead. Cool completely, uncovered, then chill, covered. When reheating, thin the soup with a little water if necessary.

Creamy Shrimp Bisque

Pat: Bisques are the most luxurious soups around. With a base of cream and seafood and brandy, they have a way of filling you and sating your appetite. This recipe is an easy, satisfying version of a dish that usually takes much longer to prepare. A quickie homemade shrimp stock provides an essential depth of flavor. And though the small amount of rice might seem unusual, it helps thicken the soup.

1 tablespoon vegetable oil

1¼ pounds medium shrimp, shelled and deveined, shells reserved

1½ cups white wine

2 quarts water

1 bay leaf

2 teaspoons salt

¼ cup butter

1 red bell pepper, diced

1 zucchini, diced

Freshly ground black pepper

1 small onion, chopped

2 celery stalks, diced

1 carrot, diced

3 tablespoons long-grain white rice

2 tablespoons tomato paste

2 tablespoons chopped fresh tarragon leaves

¼ cup brandy

¾ teaspoon cayenne pepper

½ cup heavy cream

1 tablespoon fresh lemon juice, or more to taste

Fresh chives, snipped into ½-inch lengths, for garnish

Heat the oil in a large pot over medium-high heat. Add the shrimp shells, stirring until they turn pink. Add the wine, and boil, stirring frequently, until most of the liquid has evaporated. Add the water and bay leaf and simmer, uncovered, for 20 minutes. Pour the stock through a fine sieve into a bowl, pressing on the shells to squeeze out the liquid, and then discard solids.

In a second large, heavy pot over medium-high heat, cook the shrimp with a sprinkling of salt in 1 tablespoon of the butter, stirring frequently, until they are just cooked through, 3 to 4 minutes. Using a slotted spoon, transfer the shrimp to a bowl. Add another tablespoon of the butter to the pot, and cook the bell pepper and zucchini until tender and lightly golden, about 4 minutes; transfer the vegetables to another bowl, and season lightly with salt and black pepper. Set aside.

Add the remaining 2 tablespoons of butter to the pot, then add the onion, celery, and carrot, and cook, stirring, until the vegetables are softened, 4 to 5 minutes. Stir in the rice, tomato paste, 1 tablespoon of the tarragon, the brandy, cayenne, salt, and shrimp stock, and simmer, covered, until the rice is tender, about 20 minutes. Set aside twelve shrimp, and stir the remaining shrimp into the bisque.

Purée the bisque in batches in a blender, then pour into another pot. Stir in the cream, and cook the bisque over low heat until heated through (do not boil). Stir in the lemon juice, remaining tablespoon of tarragon, and salt to taste.

Cut the reserved shrimp into ¼-inch dice, toss with the bell-pepper-and-zucchini mixture, then evenly divide among bowls as a garnish for the bisque. Top with a sprinkling of chives, and serve.

SERVES 6 TO 8

Grandma Jean's Chicken and Noodles

Gina: Few dishes are as soothing or as comforting as this creamy stew of poached chicken and tender egg noodles. As kids, when any of us were feeling low, we could always count on my mom (these days she's known as Grandma Jean) to have a pot of this soup on the stove. It seemed to me that anytime I had a bowl of it I was instantly cured. I'm not sure if it was the combination of ingredients, or the love my mother put in every pot, but I know that now, when I make it for my family, they feel the same way.

Grandma Jean would simmer a whole chicken for hours (Grandma Jean took her time with *everything*). We, however, who always seem to be pressed for time, have thankfully found a way to create similar flavors with a shortcut (don't tell Grandma!). We poach sliced chicken breasts to juicy perfection in the stock, and then add green peas and lemon juice for a final layer of fresh flavors and color. This one comes with our Neely guarantee: One bowl of this stew and you are on your way to recovery. Thanks, Mom!

---

3 tablespoons butter

3 large shallots, chopped

2 celery stalks, thinly sliced

4 ounces button mushrooms, thickly sliced

2 carrots, sliced into thin half-moons

Kosher salt

3 tablespoons all-purpose flour

6 cups Chicken Stock (page 28) or canned low-sodium chicken broth

One 10-ounce bag egg noodles

2 tablespoons vegetable oil

4 boneless, skinless chicken-breast halves, sliced diagonally into ½-inch strips

1½ cups half-and-half

One 10-ounce box frozen peas

2 tablespoons chopped fresh flat-leaf parsley or dill

Freshly ground black pepper

Melt the butter in a large pot over medium-high heat. When the butter begins to bubble, add the shallots, celery, mushrooms, carrots, and a pinch of salt, and cook until the vegetables are starting to soften, about 5 minutes. Add the flour, and cook, stirring frequently, until the vegetables are coated, about 2 minutes. Gradually stir in the chicken stock. Bring the soup to a simmer, stirring frequently, and cook until the vegetables are tender and the soup has thickened slightly, about 15 minutes.

Meanwhile, bring a large pot of water to a boil. Generously salt the water, and cook the egg noodles until they are just tender, about 7 minutes (this will vary from brand to brand, so check the bag for an accurate cooking time). Drain the noodles in a colander, transfer them to a bowl, toss them with the vegetable oil to prevent sticking, and set them aside.

Add the chicken slices to the soup pot, and simmer until the chicken is cooked through, 4 to 5 minutes. Add the half-and-half. Stir in the reserved noodles, the peas, and the parsley or dill, and simmer for another 5 minutes, until heated through. Season with salt and plenty of black pepper.

This soup can be prepared a day in advance (just allow the dish to cool slightly after cooking, then cover and refrigerate).

SERVES 6 TO 8

Vegetarian Chili

Gina: Every once in a while, my girls and I get on a little veggie kick, and they convince me to take a break from meat (amazing what a cheerleader uniform—theirs, not mine, hon—can do to you). This hearty, spicy chili is so satisfying that even Pat—my steak-and-potatoes man—loves it. The secret ingredient, bulgur (also called cracked wheat), thickens the stew when cooked and helps create a "meaty" texture. The addition of canned fire-roasted tomatoes and an unusual mix of spices gives this chili an exotic aroma and plenty of depth.

More often than not, this chili is a family affair—Spenser and Shelbi help me cut up all the colorful vegetables and tell me about their respective days, while Pat makes the cornbread that goes so well with the stew, sets the table, and privately mourns the meat that he will not be having for dinner!

---

3 tablespoons olive oil
1 onion, chopped
2 carrots, peeled and thinly sliced
1 red bell pepper, seeded and
    chopped
3 large jalapeño, seeded and
    minced (about 4½ tablespoons)
Two 28-ounce cans diced
    fire-roasted tomatoes with juice
2 cups vegetable or chicken stock
    (page 28) or water
One 15- to 16-ounce can kidney
    beans, drained
One 15- to 16-ounce can garbanzo
    beans, drained
½ cup bulgur (see note)
3 garlic cloves, minced
2 tablespoons ancho chile powder
1 tablespoon ground dried chipotle
    pepper
2 teaspoons ground cumin
1½ teaspoons ground coriander
½ teaspoon ground cinnamon
2 tablespoons red-wine vinegar
Sour cream, for garnish
Grated cheddar cheese, for garnish
Chopped fresh cilantro, for garnish

Heat the olive oil in a large pot over medium-high heat. Add the onion, carrots, bell pepper, and jalapeños, and sauté until the vegetables are almost tender, about 8 minutes. Add the tomatoes, the stock or water, beans, bulgur, garlic, chile powder, chipotle pepper, cumin, coriander, cinnamon, and vinegar, and bring to boil. Reduce the heat to low, and cook, uncovered, stirring occasionally, until the bulgur is tender and the mixture thickens, about 20 minutes. Ladle the chili into bowls, and garnish with sour cream, grated cheese, and cilantro.

SERVES 6 TO 8

NOTE: Bulgur, or cracked wheat, is available at natural-food stores and at most supermarkets (we buy ours in small amounts in the bulk-food section, so it stays fresh).

Beef and Pork Chili with Beans

Pat: Texas-style chili is all about beef, but since Memphis is all about the pigs, we give our pot a little love by adding ground pork as well. The combination of the two meats is, well, paradise for a guy like me, and it gives this chili a robust flavor and satisfying depth. Plenty of garlic, pure ground chile powder, and a bottle of beer make this one kicking combination. We call for kidney beans, but you can use black beans instead. A dollop of sour cream helps cool the fire.

4 tablespoons olive oil

2 large onions, diced

2 large red bell peppers, diced

Kosher salt

2 to 4 jalapeños, seeded and minced

6 garlic cloves, minced

1½ pounds ground pork

1½ pounds ground beef

3 tablespoons ground pure chile powder

2 tablespoons ground cumin

2 teaspoons dried oregano

2 teaspoons salt

1 teaspoon cayenne pepper

12 ounces beer

Two 28-ounce cans tomatoes with juice

2 cups beef broth

Two 15-ounce cans kidney beans, drained

Sour cream, for garnish

1 bunch scallions, thinly sliced, for garnish

Heat 2 tablespoons of the olive oil in a large skillet over medium heat. Add the onions and bell peppers and a sprinkling of salt, and sauté until the vegetables are tender, 8 to 10 minutes. Add the jalapeños and garlic and sauté for 2 more minutes; remove from the heat and set aside.

Heat the remaining 2 tablespoons olive oil in a large pot over medium-high heat. When the oil is shimmering, add the ground pork and ground beef, and sauté until browned, 10 to 15 minutes. Add the chile powder, cumin, oregano, salt, and cayenne. Reduce the heat, and cook, stirring, for about 6 minutes, until the spices form a thick paste on the meat. Add the beer, and cook, scraping up any browned bits on the bottom of the pan, for 2 to 3 minutes, until slightly reduced. Add the reserved onion-pepper mix to the pot, then the tomatoes and beef broth, and simmer for about 30 minutes.

Add the beans to the chili and cook just until they are warmed through, 3 to 4 minutes. Ladle the hot chili into bowls; top with sour cream and scallions, and serve.

SERVES 10 TO 12

NOTE: The spice tin or jar labeled "chili powder" is actually a blend of several spices, but *pure ground chile powder* is just that—one variety of dried chile that's been dried, toasted, and ground. Pure ground chile powder delivers a sharper heat and more distinct flavor. They're also bottled by the big spice companies, so they're easy to find. We like ground New Mexico, or ancho, chiles (they taste a bit like raisins and chocolate), and pure ground chipotle (which is very smoky). The variety you choose for this chili isn't terribly important; experiment and find a variety that you like best.

Nana's Southern Gumbo

We prepared this gumbo on our "Pass It On" show, because it is a generational favorite that dates back to Gina's Nana. Nana made it for Gina, Gina makes it for our daughters, and the hope is that someday our daughters will prepare it for their children. Gina and I love seafood and spicy Louisiana flavors, and this gumbo delivers plenty of both. It's delicious served over Gina's Perfect Rice (page 27). Gumbos throughout the South are made with countless combinations of seafood and meat (chicken, wild game, and spicy sausage), and ours is brimming with crab, shrimp, chicken, and ham.

½ cup vegetable oil

½ cup all-purpose flour

1 celery stalk, chopped

1 medium yellow onion, chopped

1 medium green bell pepper, chopped

2 garlic cloves, finely chopped

2 quarts Chicken Stock (page 28)

¼ cup ketchup

2 large tomatoes, chopped

1 cup cubed smoked ham (about 6 ounces)

1 pound fresh or frozen okra, sliced

¾ teaspoon salt

1 cup chopped cooked chicken (about 6 ounces)

1½ cups crabmeat (½ pound)

1 pound medium shrimp, shelled and deveined

Juice of ½ lemon

¾ teaspoon hot sauce

½ teaspoon Worcestershire sauce

In a large, heavy pot or Dutch oven, heat the oil and flour over medium-high heat, and cook, stirring constantly with a whisk, until the mixture darkens to a brown about the color of peanut butter (about 6 minutes). This is called a roux, and it will thicken the gumbo and give it a deep, rich flavor. Add the celery, onion, bell pepper, and garlic, and sauté for about 5 minutes, until the vegetables are tender.

Whisk in the stock, add the ketchup, chopped tomatoes, ham, okra, and salt, and simmer over low heat for about 1½ hours, or until the soup has thickened and the flavors are well combined. Stir in the chicken, crabmeat, and shrimp, and simmer for an additional 10 minutes, until the shrimp are fully cooked and the gumbo is warmed through. Add the lemon juice, hot sauce, and Worcestershire sauce, taste for seasonings, and serve in shallow bowls over hot steamed rice.

SERVES 6 TO 8

Hearty Beef Stew

Pat: My brothers and I have always been good eaters. As you can imagine, this meant a lot of work for our momma—feeding five hungry boys was no easy task. We all played football, and would come home after practice absolutely ravenous, ready to eat everything in the house. Lucky for us, she specialized in hearty dishes like spaghetti, lasagna, pot roast—and this rich stew. Packed with vegetables, tender beef, and a savory broth, it managed to satisfy my brothers and me . . . at least for a few hours.

When the first fall chill sets in, I find myself drawn back to Momma's cooking, so this stew remains a Neely staple (these days, however, we make it with more red wine). It's a great weekend recipe, when you've planned a day of projects around the house, because it requires only a bit of up-front work—then you get to enjoy the intoxicating smell of the stew as it simmers. Although I live in a home with three girls, don't be fooled: They hold their own when it comes to projects *and* this stew (they can polish off plenty of both). As Gina says, "Everyone has an inner pig that needs to be set free once in a while."

---

3 pounds trimmed boneless beef
   chuck, cut into 1½-inch cubes
Kosher salt
Freshly ground black pepper
6 tablespoons butter
3 tablespoons all-purpose flour
2 large onions, chopped
¼ cup tomato paste
3 cups dry red wine
Two 14½-ounce cans beef broth
1 tablespoon dark-brown sugar
1½ pounds baby red-skinned
   potatoes, quartered
One 10-ounce package baby carrots,
   rinsed
1 pound fresh cremini mushrooms,
   stemmed, caps thickly sliced
3 tablespoons whole-grain mustard
3 tablespoons chopped fresh
   flat-leaf parsley

Place the meat in a large bowl and season generously with salt and pepper. Melt 4 tablespoons of the butter in a large, heavy Dutch oven over medium-high heat. Working in batches, toss the meat with the flour; add to the pot, and brown on all sides. Using a slotted spoon, transfer the meat to a plate.

Melt the remaining 2 tablespoons butter in same pot over medium-high heat. Add the onions, and sauté until tender, about 6 minutes. Mix in the tomato paste and then the red wine. Bring to a boil, scraping up any browned bits on the bottom of the pot. Add the broth and sugar, then the browned beef and any accumulated juices. Bring to a boil; reduce the heat, and simmer, partially covered, 1½ hours, until the beef is very tender.

Add the potatoes and carrots, and simmer, uncovered, until the vegetables are tender, about 25 minutes. Add the mushrooms, mustard, and parsley; simmer until the mushrooms are tender, another 10 minutes. Season to taste with salt and pepper.

SERVES 6

Refreshing Salads

Gina: In our pig-centric world, we certainly *need* to have salads, and we crave them, too, as a refreshing complement to rich meals, and as healthful (but satisfying) meals on their own. Pat and I grew up eating salads, and, as a consequence, they have become a mainstay at our family table. (When our girls were younger, we used to call them little rabbits because they loved salads so much!) Our Nana had a garden and instilled an appreciation for fresh-flavored veggies early on. Can you imagine what that was like? Enjoying my mom's potato salad and Pat's coleslaw with Nana's fresh vegetables? You just couldn't beat it!

We've all heard the phrase "I'll just have a salad." Well, in our house, there is no "just" about salads. For us, greens are an opportunity to create a soulful, nourishing work of art. Everything goes in our salad bowl. We chop up fresh, healthful ingredients and toss them with crisp greens and fabulous dressings and have found it's as much fun and as satisfying as any other cooking experience.

We like to mix it up—showering a variety of distinctive ingredients with savory add-ins like cheese, nuts, and dried fruit. Vegetables and meats will hit the grill before the salad bowl

to infuse our salads with a smoky flavor; sweet potatoes will join the regular ones for an updated classic; and so forth. **We've even managed to sneak a little barbecue love into our salads.** Not on the lettuce, mind you (we tried—didn't work), but in the dressing. We've come up with a creamy Barbecue Ranch Dressing that you'll want to use on salads as well as sandwiches. Who said salads were dull?

Spinach Salad with Bacon, Blue Cheese, Pecans, and Cranberries

Gina: Ours is a spinach salad with some serious attitude. In addition to the bacon and creamy blue-cheese dressing, we add sweetened pecans and tart dried cranberries, and the overall effect is to give this salad a festive feel. It's a great dinner-party starter, and it's especially good partnered with a fat grilled steak. The spiced pecans are good enough to eat on their own as a snack, but try to save them for the salad! And even though we call for dried cranberries, you can substitute a variety of dried fruit, including dried cherries or golden raisins.

½ pound thick-sliced bacon strips, cut into ½-inch cubes

CREAMY BLUE-CHEESE DRESSING
4 ounces Danish blue cheese, crumbled
¼ cup buttermilk
¼ cup sour cream
Dash hot sauce
Kosher salt
Freshly ground black pepper

SALAD
One 12-ounce package baby spinach leaves
½ medium red onion, thinly sliced
1 cup dried cranberries
1 recipe Spiced Pecans (recipe follows)

Fry the bacon in a medium skillet over medium heat until brown and crisp. Using a slotted spoon, transfer the chopped bacon to a paper towel–lined plate, and set aside to cool.

To make the dressing, use a fork to mash the blue cheese in a medium bowl. Whisk in the buttermilk, sour cream, hot sauce, and salt and pepper to taste.

Combine the baby spinach, red onion, dried cranberries, bacon, and spiced pecans in a large bowl. Toss the salad with the creamy blue-cheese dressing just before serving.

SERVES 4

Spiced Pecans

Nonstick vegetable spray
¼ cup light-brown sugar
1 tablespoon olive oil
1 tablespoon balsamic vinegar
1 cup pecans
Pinch cayenne pepper

Place a 12-inch square of foil on a baking sheet, and spray the foil with nonstick vegetable spray. Heat the brown sugar, olive oil, and balsamic vinegar in a large skillet over medium heat, stirring, until the sugar melts and the mixture bubbles. Add the pecans and the cayenne, and stir until the nuts are well coated. Transfer the nuts to the foil, spreading them out, and allow them to cool completely (they will harden and dry).

MAKES 1 CUP

Chopped Salad with Barbecue Ranch Dressing

Gina: You gotta love an enormous chopped salad made with just about everything in the vegetable drawer. Our version includes the traditional ingredients of bacon, egg, and blue cheese, along with an array of colorful vegetables for fresh flavor and crunch, and our creamy Barbecue Ranch Dressing (imagine the tart, spicy creaminess of ranch with the sweetness and smoke of the barbecue sauce; it's a match made in heaven). Your vegetables will be "grooving" in the bowl! This is a hearty salad worthy of being a meal all on its own.

4 strips thick-sliced bacon
2 eggs
Kosher salt
1 bunch fresh asparagus, trimmed
1 cup chopped seedless cucumber
½ cup chopped red onion
½ cup chopped yellow bell pepper
1 cup orange (or red or yellow) grape or currant tomatoes, halved
4 ounces crumbled blue cheese
1 large head romaine lettuce, trimmed (see note) and chopped
Freshly ground black pepper

Cook the bacon in a large skillet over medium heat until crisp, then transfer to a plate lined with paper towels to cool. Bring a small saucepan of water to a gentle boil. Carefully place the eggs in the water, and simmer for 9 minutes. Drain the eggs, and rinse in cold water until cooled (the centers should still be a bit creamy). When the eggs are cool, peel and thinly slice them. Bring a large skillet of water to a boil. Add a generous pinch of salt, and blanch the asparagus until just tender, 3 to 4 minutes. Drain the asparagus, and then shock it in ice water to stop the cooking process. Drain and set aside.

You can serve this salad two ways. For the more traditional presentation, toss all of the salad ingredients with the dressing in a large bowl, and then divide among individual plates (be sure you distribute all the goodies evenly, or people will complain!). For an even prettier presentation, arrange the cucumber, onion, bell pepper, tomatoes, blue cheese, sliced eggs, and asparagus in rows, separated by color, atop the romaine lettuce on a rectangular platter or in a large, shallow serving bowl. Crumble the cooked bacon over the top, and serve the salad with Barbecue Ranch Dressing (recipe follows), allowing guests to dish up their own salad with a knife and fork on chilled individual plates. Season with pepper.

SERVES 4

NOTE: The paler inner leaves of a head of romaine are the sweetest. I trim and discard any outer leaves that are limp or bruised.

Barbecue Ranch Dressing

1 garlic clove, minced
³/₄ cup mayonnaise
¹/₂ cup buttermilk
2 tablespoons Neely's Barbecue
    Sauce (page 25)
2 teaspoons apple-cider vinegar
1 teaspoon Neely's Barbecue
    Seasoning (page 22)
³/₄ teaspoon onion powder
¹/₄ teaspoon dried dill
1 tablespoon snipped fresh chives
1 tablespoon chopped fresh flat-leaf
    parsley

Whisk the garlic, mayonnaise, buttermilk, and Neely's Barbecue Sauce together in a medium bowl. Add the vinegar, Neely's Barbecue Seasoning, onion powder, dill, chives, and parsley, and whisk until smooth. Cover and chill for 1 hour to allow flavors to meld.

MAKES 1¹/₂ CUPS

Sweet and Spicy Slaw

Pat: In Memphis, if you run a barbecue joint, you better have coleslaw on your menu and it better be good (ours is some of the very best). Indeed, you could spend a day in Memphis tasting slaw from rib joints all over town. And yet there are people who visit our fair city who

are hesitant to try it, especially folks from the West Coast. This is a mystery to me. Coleslaw and pulled pork go together like lettuce and tomatoes on a burger, and salted peanuts in a bottle of pop (I bet some of you haven't tried that, either). Bottom line: You come down Memphis way, you have to try our slaw.

When we started Neely's, Tony and I recognized the importance of slaw and knew we would have to come up with a killer recipe, one that would complement our sandwiches and our sauce. It had to be sweet yet spicy, because our barbecue sauce was truly mild. We also wanted it to be coarse and fresh (with a little onion flavor, and carrots for color). A big key for us was using two types of pepper, black and cayenne, which work together as well as Tony and I do. Then came some sugar, as sweet as my Gina. All of these ingredients have given us a coleslaw we are *very* proud of.

For years in the restaurant this was my dish—no one made it for either location but me. I didn't use measuring cups; everything was done by feel. As we grew, I knew I would eventually have to develop it into a standard recipe so others could make it. Now we have customers who come in and buy slaw by the bucket to take home and have with their catfish, spaghetti, or whatever they are cooking. This recipe will convert even those West Coast hard-liners who claim they "don't eat slaw."

Gina: On our show, we like to tease that Pat is the sweet and I am the spicy (only my man knows for sure!). At Neely's restaurants, the famous and addictive coleslaw happens to be both. We often double this recipe for parties, because leftovers are so delicious (and a food processor makes quick work of all that shredding). When making this slaw at home, it's a good idea to use both red and green cabbage. It'll give your slaw more color. Be sure to select the freshest, best-looking cabbage available for the prettiest, crispest, and crunchiest coleslaw you have ever tasted.

1 small head green cabbage
1 small head red cabbage
4 carrots
1 medium yellow onion
½ cup mayonnaise
¼ cup prepared yellow mustard
2 teaspoons apple-cider vinegar
1 cup sugar
1 teaspoon freshly ground black
    pepper
½ teaspoon cayenne pepper
Kosher salt

Cut the cabbages into quarters and remove the cores. Peel the carrots and onion, and slice them into pieces that will fit through the feed tube of a food processor. Fit the food processor with the large-holed grater attachment, and push the cabbage, carrots, and onion through the feed tube to grate. In a large bowl, toss the grated cabbage, carrots, and onions to combine.

In a medium bowl, whisk together the mayonnaise, mustard, vinegar, sugar, black pepper, and cayenne (whisk until the sugar is dissolved). Toss the dressing with the coleslaw, and season with salt and additional pepper to taste. Cover the slaw with plastic wrap, and chill for at least 2 hours before serving.

SERVES 6 TO 8

Grilled Sweet Corn Salad

When we fire up the grill to entertain, this side dish is always a big hit with our guests. Now, a lot of people grill corn on the cob for sure, but one thing our friends don't expect is for Mr. and Mrs. Barbecue to transform it into a salad (we love to surprise folks). The grilled corn imparts a wonderful smoky flavor to this salad, and the red pepper and scallions add great color and crunch. The fresh lime juice and honey create a sweet-tart dressing. This is a salad that can be prepared up to 2 days in advance, which is great for people on the go (like us)! And you may want to consider grilled sweet corn alongside most any grilled meat—including chicken, steak, or pork chops. It's the perfect accompaniment.

6 ears fresh corn, husked, silks removed
¼ cup vegetable oil
½ red bell pepper, seeds and ribs removed, finely chopped
3 scallions, white and light-green parts, trimmed and finely chopped
3 tablespoons chopped fresh cilantro or flat-leaf parsley
3 tablespoons fresh lime juice
2 tablespoons maple syrup or honey
1 teaspoon salt
¼ teaspoon freshly ground black pepper
¼ teaspoon Neely's Barbecue Seasoning (page 22)

Heat the grill to medium-high, or turn on the broiler. Brush the cobs evenly with 2 tablespoons of the oil.

When the grill is hot, grill the corn for 7 minutes, using tongs to turn the cobs as necessary for even cooking, until the corn is nicely charred on all sides. Remove the ears from the grill. (Alternatively, you can broil the corn, turning as necessary for even browning.) When the corn is cool enough to handle, use a sharp knife to strip the kernels from the cob and transfer them to a large bowl. Add the bell pepper, scallions, and cilantro or parsley.

In a small bowl, whisk together the remaining 2 tablespoons oil with the lime juice, maple syrup, salt, pepper, and Neely's Barbecue Seasoning. Pour the dressing over the corn mixture, toss well to combine, and taste to adjust seasonings (adding more salt, pepper, or lime juice as desired). Serve at room temperature.

SERVES 4 TO 6

NOTE: For an extra-smoky flavor, grill the scallions until charred and soft, 3 to 4 minutes total, then finely chop.

Two-Potato Salad with Creole Mustard, Bacon, and Arugula

Here's a more contemporary take on potato salad: Two kinds of potatoes give it eye appeal and a richer flavor. Tossing the potatoes with arugula and bacon adds a peppery crunch and plenty of smoky goodness (and you know how we feel about the smoke!)—and practically makes this salad a meal. Because sweet potatoes are so dense, and they take a few minutes longer to cook than regular potatoes, we cook them separately. This salad doubles easily for a party, and goes great with barbecued brisket or grilled sausages.

4 strips thick-sliced smoked bacon
1 pound sweet potatoes, peeled and
　　cut into 1-inch cubes
1 pound Yukon Gold potatoes,
　　peeled and cut into 1-inch cubes
1 teaspoon kosher salt
4 scallions, finely chopped
2 celery stalks, finely chopped
2 serrano chiles, stemmed, seeded,
　　and minced
½ cup plus 2 tablespoons
　　mayonnaise
2 tablespoons Creole mustard
　　(see note)
1 tablespoon finely chopped fresh
　　tarragon leaves
Freshly ground black pepper
6 ounces arugula

Fry the bacon in a large skillet over medium heat until crisp and browned. Transfer the bacon to a plate lined with paper towels and set aside.

Place the sweet potatoes and Yukon Gold potatoes in two separate saucepans. Cover the potatoes with water (by 2 inches), add ½ teaspoon salt to each pot, and bring the pots to a boil over medium-high heat. Reduce the heat, and simmer the potatoes until they are just cooked through and tender. The sweet potatoes will cook in about 15 minutes, and the Yukon Gold potatoes should be finished in about 12 minutes. Drain the potatoes, and allow them to cool.

Combine the potatoes, scallions, celery, and serrano chiles in a large bowl. Add the mayonnaise, mustard, tarragon, salt, and pepper, and combine. Taste for seasoning, and add more salt or pepper, as desired. Toss the potato salad with the arugula, and serve on a large platter, garnished with the crumbled bacon.

SERVES 6 TO 8

NOTE: Creole mustard is a whole-grain mustard with a creamy texture and a zippy horseradish flavor. In other words, it's a mustard with a little extra kick, so it's right up our alley!

Five Bean Picnic Salad

Gina: This colorful salad is one of my go-to recipes when I need something to satisfy a crowd, whether at a church potluck supper or a backyard barbecue. The champagne vinaigrette gives the beans a fresh, zippy flavor. For the best results, add the fresh beans to the salad just before serving, so they do not discolor.

Kosher salt

¾ pound green beans, trimmed
and halved

¾ pound yellow wax beans,
trimmed and halved

One 14-ounce can dark-red kidney
beans, drained and rinsed

One 14-ounce can black-eyed peas,
drained and rinsed

One 14-ounce can garbanzo beans,
drained and rinsed

1 bunch scallions, white and
light-green parts, thinly sliced

1 red (or orange or yellow) bell
pepper, diced

2 tablespoons chopped fresh
flat-leaf parsley leaves, for
garnish

2 tablespoons chopped fresh
marjoram or oregano leaves
(optional)

1 recipe Champagne Vinaigrette
(recipe follows)

Freshly ground black pepper

Hot sauce

Bring a large pot of water to a boil. Add a generous sprinkling of salt and the fresh beans, and cook until the beans are just tender, about 8 minutes. Drain the beans in a colander, and shock in ice water to stop the cooking process. Drain again and set aside.

Place the fresh and canned beans, scallions, bell pepper, parsley, marjoram, and Champagne Vinaigrette in a large bowl, and toss to combine. Season the salad to taste with salt, pepper, and hot sauce.

SERVES 6 TO 8

Champagne Vinaigrette

1 garlic clove, finely chopped

2 tablespoons Dijon mustard

¼ cup champagne vinegar

2 tablespoons fresh lemon juice

2 tablespoons honey

2 or 3 dashes hot sauce

½ teaspoon salt

½ teaspoon freshly ground black
  pepper

½ cup extra-virgin olive oil

Whisk together the garlic, mustard, vinegar, lemon juice, honey, hot sauce, salt, and pepper in a large bowl. Slowly whisk in the olive oil until the dressing has emulsified. Alternatively, you can combine all the ingredients in a blender or a food processor and purée until smooth.

MAKES ¾ CUP

Green Bean Salad with Nutty Basil Dressing

A pesto-like dressing made from walnuts, garlic, and plenty of fragrant basil gives fresh, tender green beans a vibrant flavor. This simple, satisfying salad is delicious alongside grilled burgers, roasted chicken, or pan-seared fish.

½ cup walnuts
Kosher salt
1½ pounds green beans, trimmed
1 garlic clove
½ cup fresh basil leaves
2 tablespoons Dijon mustard
3 tablespoons red-wine vinegar
1 tablespoon honey
5 tablespoons extra-virgin olive oil
1 pint cherry tomatoes, halved
½ red onion, thinly sliced
Freshly ground black pepper

Preheat the oven to 400°F. Place the walnuts on a baking sheet and toast in the oven until fragrant and slightly darker, 7 to 8 minutes. Set the nuts aside to cool.

Bring a large pot of water to a boil. Add a generous sprinkling of salt, then the green beans, and boil until they are just tender, about 8 minutes. Drain the beans in a colander, and shock in ice water to stop the cooking process.

Combine the walnuts, garlic, basil, mustard, vinegar, and honey in the bowl of a food processor fitted with a metal blade. Purée the ingredients until a rough paste forms. With the processor running, add the olive oil in a slow stream until the dressing is smooth and emulsified.

Place the beans and the dressing in a large bowl, and toss until combined. Add the tomatoes and onion and toss again. Taste the salad, and season with additional salt and freshly ground pepper, as desired. Serve immediately, or cover with plastic and refrigerate until needed.

SERVES 4 TO 6

NOTE: For a nuttier flavor, replace 1 tablespoon of the olive oil with walnut oil.

Grandma Jean's Potato Salad

Gina: Wow, life sure has a way of kicking you in the stomach when you least expect it. Ladies, I am sure you will understand what I'm talking about. You know that person who's been in your life all along and you've never really seen him? That's how it was with Pat and me. His mom and my mom went to school together, his brothers and my sisters were classmates, and, yes, you guessed it, we went to the same high school. . . . Sometimes the best things in life are right in front of you (if you keep your eyes open).

That's how I feel about my mom's potato salad. She always made it for us when we were kids, but I didn't truly appreciate it until I moved away. What is it they say about absence and the heart? That's when I knew I had to master this recipe on my own. The first time I prepared it for Pat, he recognized that this was one apple that hadn't fallen far from the tree. This potato salad remains a standout at all of our big family gatherings. Even if Mom can't make it to an event, her potato salad will always be there!

I think the creamy red potatoes, sweet-pickle relish, and sharp yellow mustard give this salad a distinct flavor and an appetizing color. Pat loves the richness that the big chunks of hard-boiled egg provide (and the way a little sugar brings out the flavors of the other ingredients).

5 large red potatoes (2 pounds), cubed
Kosher salt
1 medium onion, finely chopped
2 celery stalks, finely chopped
3 hard-boiled eggs, 2 chopped and 1 sliced
One 10-ounce jar sweet-pickle relish, drained
2 tablespoons Miracle Whip
1 tablespoon prepared yellow mustard
1 tablespoon sugar
Paprika, for garnish

Bring a large pot of water to a boil. Add the cubed potatoes and a generous pinch of salt, and cook until the potatoes are tender, about 15 minutes. Drain the potatoes in a colander, and cool. In a large bowl, combine the onion, celery, 2 chopped eggs, pickle relish, Miracle Whip, yellow mustard, sugar, and salt to taste. Using a rubber spatula, fold in the potatoes. Transfer the salad to a serving container, top with the sliced egg, and sprinkle with paprika. Cover the salad with plastic wrap, and refrigerate for at least 1 hour, or overnight for the fullest flavor.

SERVES 6

Grilled Lemon Chicken Salad with Potatoes and Pistachios

A plain old grilled chicken breast can be a bit uninspired, so we like to jazz up our breasts (who said that?) in this version of grilled chicken salad that has plenty of moxie. The marinade of fresh lemon juice and zest, olive oil, and fresh herbs infuses the chicken with a bright, sunny flavor (so yummy that you'll want to use the marinade again and again for grilled meats).

Here we team the grilled chicken with potatoes, celery, green olives, pistachios, and a creamy mayonnaise dressing for an over-the-top texture-and-flavor combination. This recipe doubles or triples beautifully, so it's great for special lunches (think birthday parties, anniversaries, or bridal showers). It's also great with a glass of chilled white wine and a crackly baguette.

CHICKEN

3 tablespoons chopped fresh thyme
    leaves
2 teaspoons grated lemon zest
1/2 cup olive oil
3 tablespoons fresh lemon juice
1 large shallot, finely chopped
2 garlic cloves, minced
Kosher salt
Freshly ground black pepper
Pinch crushed red-pepper flakes
4 skinless, boneless chicken-breast
    halves

SALAD

1 pound Yukon Gold potatoes,
    unpeeled, cut into 1/2-inch cubes
Kosher salt
Freshly ground black pepper
3 tablespoons mayonnaise
3 tablespoons sour cream
2 tablespoons chopped fresh mint
    leaves
1 teaspoon grated lemon zest
1 tablespoon fresh lemon juice

Combine the thyme, lemon zest, olive oil, lemon juice, shallot, garlic, salt and pepper, and red-pepper flakes in a 1-gallon Ziploc bag. Add the chicken to the bag, seal it, and gently massage the ingredients to combine. Marinate the chicken at room temperature for 1 hour, or chill for up to 8 hours, massaging and turning the bag occasionally.

Place the potatoes in a medium saucepan and cover with water by 2 inches. Add a pinch of salt, bring the water to a boil, reduce the heat, and simmer the potatoes until tender, 12 to 14 minutes. Drain the potatoes in a colander, and then place them in a large bowl. Season the potatoes with salt and pepper.

Combine the mayonnaise, sour cream, mint, lemon zest, and lemon juice in a small bowl; whisk to blend, and then season the dressing with salt and pepper. Cover, and chill until ready to use.

Heat the grill or a grill pan to medium-high. Remove the chicken from the marinade, and grill the breasts until golden brown and cooked through, 5 to 6 minutes per side (do not overcook). Transfer the chicken to a work surface, and let cool for 15 minutes. Cut the chicken into 1/2-inch cubes; add to the potatoes in the bowl, and then mix in the celery, olives, and dressing until well combined. Season to taste with salt and

3 celery stalks, thinly sliced

1 cup coarsely chopped brine-cured green olives

⅓ cup coarsely chopped shelled roasted, salted pistachios

pepper. Transfer the salad to a serving platter, top with the chopped pistachios, and serve immediately.

You can also chill this salad up to a day in advance, but hold off on adding the pistachios until just before serving (so they won't get soft in the fridge), and you'll want to bring the salad to room temperature before serving.

SERVES 6

Stick-to-Your-Ribs Side Dishes

Gina: Side dishes are like a great accessory to a fabulous outfit—they have to be just right or else the outfit is *not working*. So you need to plan your side dishes carefully, and think about how they will play out with the rest of the meal.

For instance, what would a slab of ribs be without brimming bowls of creamy potato salad, crunchy coleslaw, and sweet, smoky baked beans on the side? And can you imagine serving a sauce or gravy dish without fluffy white rice or a wedge of warm cornbread to mop up the juices? Even roasts become more enticing when they are joined with a serving of glazed root vegetables, collard greens, or okra with tomatoes. Traditionally, Southern side dishes are based on inexpensive staples that are easy to prepare—that's our idea of keeping it real and delicious!

Most folks might consider serving two or three sides, along with a green salad, sufficient, but here in the South, honey, you may have to plate up four or five different sides, because we can have trouble paring things down—and as a result end up preparing them all! Adding one or two of the following recipes to any meal (a basic roasted chicken or a grilled burger, for instance) will turn it into a feast. Our family favorites rely on the South's most beloved ingredients—sweet potatoes, okra, black-eyed peas, leafy greens, corn, green beans, and good old pork fat, of course (did you think we were going to leave out the pig?).

Southern Creamed Corn

Gina: Pat and I are huge fans of grilled corn on the cob, but once the girls started wearing braces (!) we had to figure out a better—easier to eat—alternative, for obvious reasons. Shucked corn in cream did the trick. After a while, the girls became accustomed to having corn served in this decadent manner, and pretty soon there was no turning back. Thus, another Neely staple was born. I think the sweetness that this method coaxes from the fresh corn makes all the difference in the world, and I know Pat agrees. When my husband serves us this dish, he always says, "Some sweet for my sweets."

8 ears corn, husked
2 tablespoons sugar
1 tablespoon all-purpose flour
Kosher salt
Freshly ground black pepper
Pinch cayenne pepper
1 cup heavy cream
½ cup cold water
2 tablespoons bacon fat
1 tablespoon butter

Use one hand to hold an ear of corn at a 45-degree angle, with one end of the cob resting on a cutting board; then use a knife to trim the kernels. After all the kernels have been stripped from the ear, rest it over a bowl and, using a butter knife, scrape the blade against the cob, pressing out the milky liquid. Repeat with the remaining ears of corn.

Whisk together the sugar, flour, salt, black pepper, and cayenne in a small bowl. Sprinkle the dry ingredients over the corn kernels, and toss to combine. Add the heavy cream and water to the corn, and stir to combine.

Heat the bacon fat in a large skillet over medium heat until it is very hot but not smoking. Add the corn mixture, and stir until the mixture sizzles; reduce the heat to medium-low, and cook, stirring occasionally, until the mixture becomes thick and creamy, about 30 minutes. Stir in the butter, taste for seasonings, and add additional salt and pepper, as desired.

SERVES 6 TO 8

Use one hand to hold the corn, then use a sharp knife to trim the kernels from the cob (to keep your fingers safe, always slice away from you). Once the kernels are stripped from the cob, use a butter knife to scrape out the milky liquid.

Seared Okra and Tomatoes

Pat: Few flavor combinations sing "summertime in the South" more than okra and tomatoes. Some people find okra intimidating to cook, but it's really very simple. If okra is cooked for too long over too low a heat, it can turn slimy and limp. The secret is first searing the okra over a very high heat, then finishing it for a few minutes in the piquant tomato sauce. This method prevents the okra from getting gooey (frying okra does the same thing). Okra and tomatoes are great alongside fried fish, or any roasted or grilled meat, and they also pair well over a creamy starch like grits or spoonbread.

3 tablespoons olive oil

1 medium onion, diced

3 garlic cloves, thinly sliced

2 tablespoons tomato paste

One 14-ounce can diced tomatoes with juice

½ teaspoon salt

½ teaspoon black pepper

1 teaspoon chopped fresh rosemary leaves

½ teaspoon crushed red-pepper flakes

2 bay leaves

2 tablespoons red-wine vinegar

1⅓ cups Chicken Stock (page 28)

1½ pounds okra, cut into 1½-inch-thick slices (about 3 cups)

Heat 1 tablespoon of the olive oil in a medium skillet over medium-high heat. When the oil is hot, add the onion and garlic, and sauté for 2 minutes. Add the tomato paste, diced tomatoes, salt, pepper, rosemary, red-pepper flakes, bay leaves, and vinegar, and cook for 10 minutes, until the tomatoes start to break down and form a paste. Add the chicken stock, return to a simmer, and cook over low heat for 10 to 15 minutes, stirring occasionally.

While the tomato sauce cooks, heat the remaining 2 tablespoons of olive oil in a large skillet over medium-high heat. When the oil is very hot and shimmering, sauté the okra for about 5 minutes, until lightly browned, then add the okra to the tomato sauce. Simmer the okra-tomato mixture for 2 to 3 more minutes, remove the bay leaves, and then serve.

SERVES 4 TO 6

Sautéed Kale with Onion and Bacon

Gina: Some Southern greens benefit from long, slow cooking, but kale is best prepared as a speedy sauté. Shredding the kale allows it to cook even faster, keeping its bright color and abundant nutrients (calcium, vitamins A and C) intact. Adding bacon, onion, and the unexpected flavor of smoked Spanish paprika creates a spectacular side dish that just might steal the show from the main course. For a quick, satisfying dinner, you could also toss this sauté with whole-wheat pasta, and finish the dish with toasted pine nuts and grated Parmesan cheese.

2½ pounds (about 4 bunches) kale, tough stems and center ribs cut off and discarded
2 tablespoons olive oil
4 strips thick-sliced bacon, cut into ½-inch pieces
1 large onion, thinly sliced
4 garlic cloves, thinly sliced
Generous pinch crushed red-pepper flakes
¼ teaspoon smoked Spanish paprika
1 cup Chicken Stock (page 28) or water
2 teaspoons sherry-wine vinegar
Kosher salt
Freshly ground black pepper

Stack a few kale leaves and roll them lengthwise into a cigar shape. Cut the leaves crosswise into ¼-inch-wide strips with a sharp knife. Repeat with the remaining kale leaves. (See note.)

Heat the olive oil in a wide 6- to 8-quart pot over moderate heat. Add the bacon, and cook, stirring occasionally, until browned but still soft, then use a slotted spoon to transfer the bacon to a plate lined with paper towels to drain. Pour off and discard all but 3 tablespoons of oil and fat from the pot, and then add the onion, garlic, and red-pepper flakes, and cook over low heat, stirring, until softened, 5 to 7 minutes. Add the kale, bacon, and smoked paprika to the pot, and cook, turning with tongs, until the kale is wilted and bright green, about 1 minute. Add the stock or water and simmer, partially covered, until the leaves are just tender, 6 to 10 minutes. Add the vinegar, and toss to combine; taste for seasonings, and add salt, pepper, or more vinegar as desired.

SERVES 8

NOTES: Large kale leaves are easier to cut in the manner described in this recipe. If all you can find are small leaves, just coarsely chop them.

Smoked Spanish paprika, also called *pimentón,* has an entirely different flavor from regular paprika. It is really, really smoky—and a little goes a long way in any dish.

Broccoli Cheddar Cornbread

Pat: Broccoli in cornbread—who knew? But sometimes you need to go to great lengths, and be very crafty, to get your kids to eat more vegetables. The result in this instance is a moist, incredibly satisfying cornbread that gets added richness from both cottage and cheddar cheese. We call for frozen broccoli, which makes this recipe easy enough to whip together in the time it takes your oven to preheat. (You can also use 2½ cups of fresh steamed broccoli.)

½ cup unsalted butter

1 medium onion, chopped

2 garlic cloves, minced

One 10-ounce package frozen chopped broccoli, thawed but not drained (or see headnote)

Two 8½-ounce boxes cornbread mix

½ cup whole milk

One 8-ounce container cottage cheese

4 large eggs

1 tablespoon salt

1 cup plus 2 tablespoons grated sharp cheddar cheese, for topping

Preheat the oven to 375°F.

Heat the butter in a 10-inch cast-iron skillet over medium-high heat. Add the onion, and sauté until softened, 4 to 5 minutes. Add the garlic and broccoli to the skillet, and sauté for 2 minutes, until the garlic is fragrant and the broccoli has warmed through. In a medium bowl, stir together the cornbread mix, milk, cottage cheese, eggs, salt, and 1 cup of the cheddar cheese until smooth, then pour the batter into the skillet over the vegetables and stir to blend. Sprinkle the top of the batter with the remaining cheese. Bake the cornbread in the skillet for about 30 minutes, until it is lightly golden and a toothpick inserted in the center comes out clean. Cool for 5 to 10 minutes, then serve.

SERVES 6

Fried Green Tomatoes with Basil Mayonnaise

Gina: Who would think that a hard green tomato would yield such tender, irresistible results? Coated with cornmeal and bread crumbs, fried to crispy perfection, and served warm with an awesome basil mayo, fried green tomatoes are delicious atop field greens or butter lettuce, or on toasted sandwiches with a few fried strips of bacon.

6 hard green tomatoes, sliced
    ¼ inch thick
Kosher salt
Freshly ground black pepper
¾ cup all-purpose flour
¾ cup well-shaken buttermilk
Dash hot sauce
¾ cup yellow cornmeal
1½ cups Japanese panko bread
    crumbs
Vegetable oil, for frying
1 recipe Basil Mayonnaise
    (recipe follows)

Season the tomatoes with salt and pepper. Place the flour on a plate. Whisk together the buttermilk and hot sauce in a shallow bowl or a pie tin. Whisk together the cornmeal and panko bread crumbs in a separate pie tin.

Working with one green-tomato slice at a time, coat the tomato first in flour (knocking off excess), then in the buttermilk, then finally in the cornmeal–bread crumb mixture. Transfer the breaded slice to a baking sheet, and repeat with the remaining slices.

Preheat the oven to 200°F. Line a second baking sheet with paper towels.

Heat ¾ inch of vegetable oil in a medium skillet to 350°F. Working in batches, fry the tomato slices until golden brown, about 2 minutes per side. Using a slotted spoon, transfer the cooked tomatoes to the prepared baking sheet, and sprinkle with salt and pepper. Keep the cooked tomatoes in the warm oven while you fry the remaining slices. Serve the tomatoes warm, with a generous dollop of Basil Mayonnaise.

SERVES 6

Basil Mayonnaise

2 cups loosely packed fresh basil
    leaves
1 cup mayonnaise
2 tablespoons fresh lemon juice
1 tablespoon Creole mustard
    (see page 93)
Kosher salt
Freshly ground black pepper

Pulse the basil, mayonnaise, lemon juice, and mustard in a food processor fitted with a metal blade until smooth, then transfer to small bowl. Season with salt and pepper.

The Basil Mayonnaise can be made 1 day ahead. Cover and refrigerate.

MAKES ABOUT 1¼ CUPS

Braised Cabbage and Carrots

Gina: This simple, satisfying braise is another Neely staple. After a bit of knife work in the beginning, most of the cooking is unattended, and I love the aroma of bacon and cabbage while I set the table or simply hang with a glass of wine and my girls. Baby carrots add a contemporary twist to this otherwise old-fashioned dish, and they're a nice color accent for the cabbage. Homemade Smash Seasoning and fresh parsley have the effect of punching up the flavors.

1 large head green cabbage
4 slices extra-thick bacon, cut into
   1-inch pieces
1 large onion, diced
Kosher salt
Freshly ground black pepper
1 recipe Smash Seasoning (recipe
   follows)
One 10-ounce bag baby carrots
   (or regular carrots, peeled and
   sliced on the bias into
   ½-inch-thick coins)
3 tablespoons chopped fresh
   flat-leaf parsley (optional)

Core the cabbage and slice it into 2-inch squares. Thoroughly rinse the cabbage under running water, and then drain in a colander. Cook the bacon in a large pot over medium-high heat until it has rendered much of its fat and is lightly browned but still moist (do not drain the fat). Add the onion and a generous pinch of salt and pepper, and cook, stirring, for another 5 to 7 minutes, until the onion is softened. Add the cabbage, 1 cup water, and the Smash Seasoning to the pot. Bring the mixture to a boil, reduce the heat to low, then cover and braise for about 1 hour, stirring occasionally, until the cabbage is tender.

Add the carrots. Cover and cook for another hour, stirring occasionally, until the carrots are tender. Stir in the parsley, taste for seasonings, and add more salt and pepper, as desired.

SERVES 4 TO 6

Smash Seasoning

1 teaspoon cayenne pepper
1 teaspoon celery seed
½ tablespoon lemon pepper
1 tablespoon garlic powder

Stir together the ingredients in a small bowl.

Three Ways to Skin a Cat

Gina: YOU KNOW THE SAYING "There's more than one way to skin a cat"? Well, my Nana used to say, "You gotta hit a man three ways to get him." The three ways are the head, the stomach, and the lower part (you know what I'm talkin' about). Well, I had two out of three taken care of, so I had to get to that belly. The first night I invited Pat over for dinner—I remember as if it was yesterday—I served spicy fried chicken, collard greens, macaroni and cheese, my momma's potato salad, and cornbread. And then, for dessert, I made him my Candy Bar Brownie Crunch (page 202) with marshmallows. *Girl,* that man almost had a heart attack! But he did live through the night, and the rest, as they say, is history. Honeys, if you are trying to get a man, always remember what my Nana said—get him three ways!

Pat always saw me as this little "prissy" girl in high school. You know the kind: looks good, smells good, dresses cute, and can't boil water! So I'm sure he was shocked to see how I had grown—and that I knew my way around the kitchen! After Pat and I "reunited" at our high-school reunion, when I returned to Memphis from California, I was a woman on a mission: I was going to work my man ovah!

Gina's Collard Greens

Gina: I'm always surprised to discover that folks in these parts tend to cook turnip and mustard greens more often than collard greens. I think the perception is that collards tend to be a little bitter. But I gotta tell you, you're sleeping on this one! Rich in vitamins and nutrients, collard greens are actually the sweetest, best-tasting leaves you can buy (turnip and mustard greens, on the other hand, have a slightly spicy, peppery taste). In this recipe, the deep, full flavor of the collard greens along with a bit of sugar and some heat from the red-pepper flakes create an irresistible sweet-and-hot pot of goodness, while the ham hocks add a note of smoke that balances out the other flavors. Pat can't get enough of these sweet greens. Trust me on this one, ladies—this is the recipe that'll bring your man home every night!

Five bunches of collards might seem like a lot of greens, but these jokers will cook down to a fraction of their original size.

---

5 bunches collard greens (about 3 pounds)
3 ham hocks
¼ cup salt
1 cup sugar
1½ teaspoons crushed red-pepper flakes

Using your hands, pull the leaves from the thick collard greens stems, and discard the stems. Roll the leaves lengthwise into a cigar shape, and cut crosswise into large pieces. Fill a clean sink or a large pot with plenty of cold water, and rinse the greens in the water, allowing any dirt or grit to sink to the bottom (repeat several times with fresh water, if necessary). Lift the greens out of the water, and set aside in a colander to drain.

Heat the ham hocks, salt, and 3 cups water in a large pot over medium-high heat. Bring the water to a boil, reduce the heat to low, and simmer until the ham hocks are slightly tender, about 30 minutes. Add the greens, sugar, and red-pepper flakes to the pot, stirring to combine. Cover the pot, and continue cooking over low heat, stirring occasionally, until the greens are tender, about 45 minutes. If the pot gets too dry, add more water as necessary to keep the greens moist (you'll want to serve the greens with a generous amount of the flavorful cooking liquid).

SERVES 6 TO 8

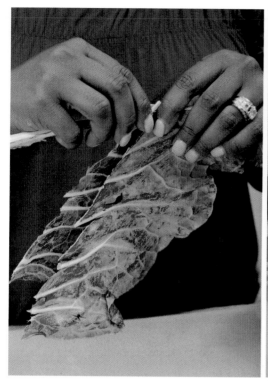

It's easy to use your fingers to strip the succulent leaves from the thick stems. Rolling the leaves into a tight cigar shape makes for easier slicing.

Cheesy Corkscrews with Crunchy Bacon Topping

Pat: When I was growing up in Memphis, everyone had their own special mac-and-cheese recipe. Traditionally, the matriarchs used elbow noodles, but my girls love experimenting with different pasta, and we fell in love with cavatappi, because its tubular spiral shape holds plenty of cheese sauce, making every forkful a delight (of course, old-fashioned elbows will also work just fine).

A piquant, cheesy white sauce and a crispy topping made from potato chips and bacon creates the best—and most indulgent—version of mac and cheese that we have ever tasted. Served alongside roast chicken, or with a simple green salad and a glass of great red wine, this is the ultimate comfort food.

CHEESY CORKSCREWS

6 tablespoons butter, plus more
  for greasing
Kosher salt
1 pound cavatappi (or other tubular
  pasta)
½ cup all-purpose flour
4 cups whole milk, warmed
1 teaspoon dry mustard powder
1 teaspoon salt
¼ teaspoon freshly ground black
  pepper
¼ teaspoon cayenne pepper
Pinch freshly grated nutmeg
Dash hot sauce
Dash Worcestershire sauce
4 cups grated sharp white cheddar
  cheese
1¼ cups grated Pecorino Romano
  cheese

CRUNCHY BACON TOPPING

1½ cups crushed potato chips
½ cup grated Pecorino Romano
  cheese
5 slices cooked bacon, crumbled
3 tablespoons chopped fresh
  flat-leaf parsley

Heat the oven to 375°F. Butter a 3-quart casserole dish.

Bring a large pot of generously salted water to a boil, and cook the pasta until it's al dente. Melt the butter in a large saucepan over medium heat. Add the flour, and cook, stirring, for 1 minute. Whisk in the warmed milk, and bring to a simmer, whisking constantly (the mixture will thicken as the heat increases).

Stir the dry mustard, salt, black pepper, cayenne, nutmeg, hot sauce, and Worcestershire sauce into the thickened milk. Stir in 3 cups of the cheddar, and the Pecorino Romano, until the cheeses melt.

Add the cooked pasta to the cheese sauce, and toss to combine. Pour the cheese-apalooza mixture into the prepared casserole dish.

Make the topping: In a medium bowl, combine the potato chips, Pecorino Romano, crumbled bacon, parsley, and the remaining cheddar. Sprinkle the crumb mixture on top of the macaroni and cheese, and bake for 35 minutes. For a crunchier topping, finish under the broiler for 3 minutes, until golden brown and crisp. Remove from the oven, and cool for 5 minutes before serving.

SERVES 6 TO 8

Cheesy Potato Casserole

Pat: Good old mashed (or fried) potatoes are an everyday event in the South, but there's something about a casserole of cheesy scalloped potatoes that makes a meal more special. After experimenting with countless variations, we decided that this two-cheese version was our favorite. You'll love how the sharp cheddar mingles with the blue cheese, and how the finished casserole has a crispy top and a tender, creamy middle. This dish has become a Neely holiday staple, especially at Thanksgiving, because it's delicious with turkey and buttered green beans.

4 tablespoons butter, plus more for greasing
1¼ cups (packed) grated extra-sharp cheddar cheese (about 6 ounces)
¾ cup crumbled Danish blue cheese (about 4 ounces)
4 pounds russet potatoes, peeled, cut into ¼-inch-thick rounds (see note)
1½ teaspoons salt
½ teaspoon freshly ground black pepper
1 bunch scallions, finely chopped
3 tablespoons all-purpose flour
3 cups whole milk
¼ teaspoon freshly grated dried nutmeg
Generous pinch cayenne pepper

Preheat the oven to 400°F. Lightly butter a 13 × 9 × 2-inch glass baking dish.

Mix the cheddar cheese and blue cheese in a small bowl.

Arrange half of the sliced potatoes in the prepared baking dish, overlapping slightly. Sprinkle the potatoes with a teaspoon of the salt and ¼ teaspoon of the black pepper. Sprinkle the scallions over the potatoes, and then dust them with the flour and dot with 2 tablespoons of the butter. Sprinkle half of the cheese mixture over the potatoes. Top with the remaining potatoes, ½ teaspoon salt, ¼ teaspoon black pepper, and 2 tablespoons butter.

Reserve the remaining cheese.

Bring the milk, nutmeg, and cayenne to a simmer in a medium saucepan. Pour the milk over the potatoes (it will not cover them completely). Cover the dish tightly with foil, and bake for 45 minutes. Remove the baking dish from the oven, uncover, and sprinkle the potatoes with the reserved cheese. Bake, uncovered, until the potatoes are tender and the cheese is deep golden brown, about 45 minutes longer. Remove the dish from the oven; let the casserole stand for 15 minutes before serving.

SERVES 12

NOTE: An inexpensive plastic Japanese mandoline makes quick work of slicing the potatoes. This casserole can be prepared up to a day in advance. Rewarm, covered, in a 375°F oven for about 20 minutes.

Cornbread Stuffing with Oysters and Andouille

Pat: In the South, most stuffing recipes call for some kind of meat, whether it's bacon, liver, chicken, or boiled turkey, as well as some kind of stock to keep the stuffing moist.

In this recipe, the briny oysters meld beautifully with the spicy andouille sausage, and the end result is a stuffing so good that you won't want to wait until Thanksgiving to try it. For the best results, use day-old cornbread, so it has time to dry out a bit, which will enable it to absorb all the flavorful juices inside the bird.

---

1 recipe Crusty Cornbread (page 29), or two 8½ ounce boxes cornbread mix, prepared as directed, and cut into 1-inch cubes (about 8 cups)

2 tablespoons vegetable oil, plus more for greasing

½ pound andouille sausage, sliced into ½-inch half-moons

1 medium onion, finely chopped

3 celery stalks, finely chopped

1 red bell pepper, finely chopped

2 jalapeños, seeded and minced

3 cups Chicken Stock (page 28)

3 large eggs, lightly beaten

1 pint shucked oysters, drained and coarsely chopped

1 bunch scallions, coarsely chopped

½ cup chopped fresh flat-leaf parsley leaves

2 teaspoons salt

1½ teaspoons black pepper

¼ to ½ teaspoon cayenne pepper

1½ teaspoons poultry seasoning

½ teaspoon dried oregano

1 tablespoon chopped fresh thyme leaves

Set aside the prepared and cubed cornbread.

Grease a 9 × 13-inch baking dish with vegetable oil.

Heat the vegetable oil in a large skillet over medium heat. Add the andouille, onion, celery, bell pepper, and jalapeños to the skillet, and cook, stirring, for 5 to 8 minutes, until the vegetables begin to soften. Remove the skillet from the heat and set it aside.

Preheat the oven to 350°F.

In a large mixing bowl, combine the cornbread with the stock, then add the cooked vegetables, the eggs, oysters, scallions, parsley, salt, cayenne pepper, poultry seasoning, oregano, and thyme. Using your hands, mix all the ingredients together to combine. Transfer the cornbread mixture to the prepared baking dish, cover with foil, and bake for 1 hour. Remove the baking dish from the oven, uncover, and bake for an additional 20 minutes, until the top of the stuffing is golden brown and crusty. Remove the dish from the oven, and let sit for at least 15 minutes before serving.

Leftovers will keep in the refrigerator for 1 or 2 days.

SERVES 10 TO 12

Smoky New Potatoes and Green Beans

Gina: Green beans and new potatoes, simmered with some type of pork fat, are a classic Southern combination. This dish is one we both grew up on, and when we cook it at home, the smoky aroma of these simmering vegetables instantly transports us to our mothers' kitchens. There are few flavors more satisfying to any Southerner than the taste of tender new potatoes and green beans that have absorbed the salty, porky goodness of a smoked ham hock.

2 smoked ham hocks

2 pounds green beans, stem ends trimmed

½ cup sugar (or less to taste; see note)

2 teaspoons kosher salt

2 pounds small red new potatoes, rinsed and trimmed of any imperfections

1 recipe Smash Seasoning (page 112)

Freshly ground black pepper

Hot sauce, for serving (optional)

Place the ham hocks in a large pot, and add enough water just to cover, then bring the water to a boil. Reduce the heat to low, cover, and simmer for 1½ hours, skimming any scum that rises to the surface, until the ham hocks are very tender and the meat is falling away from the bone. Add the green beans, sugar, and salt to the pot and continue cooking, stirring occasionally, for another 25 minutes. Add the potatoes and Smash Seasoning to the pot, and cook until the potatoes are tender, about 20 minutes more.

Remove the ham hocks from the pot. Discard the leathery skin (it should pull off easily), and, using a fork, pull the meat from the bone. Coarsely chop the meat, and add it back to the pot. Taste for seasonings, and then serve with hot sauce, if desired.

SERVES 6 TO 8

NOTE: Only a Yankee would consider draining the magnificent cooking liquid known as "pot liquor" from this dish. We definitely like ours on the sweeter side, so if you don't, feel free to use less sugar or leave it out altogether. If you want a neater presentation, go ahead and use a slotted spoon to transfer the potatoes and beans to a serving dish, but to enjoy them "down home" style, serve them in a shallow bowl with plenty of cooking liquid, several dashes of hot sauce, and warm, buttered cornbread on the side for sopping up every last drop of goodness.

Ham Hocks

Gina: **A HAM HOCK** is the shank end of the leg bone of a smoked ham, and they have always been a staple in Momma Callie's pot. I can't recall a time in my childhood when they weren't simmering (and imparting their rich, smoky goodness) with a pot of greens and other vegetables (especially green beans, cabbage, and white beans). Back in those days, all home cooks used them, so I learned to do what the *real* divas did, and now I add them to my pots as well. My older sister Kim used to get on me because I would throw away the hocks after they'd cooked. "You don't know what you're missin', hon!" Kim would peel off the skin and eat all of the moist, smoky meat. Lord, I *was* missing out (now I chop all that moist meat and add it back into the pot). I know

a lot of younger cooks use smoked-turkey parts these days, but—you know what?—if it ain't broke, don't fix it. I am a firm believer in the old-school way, so in the end I choose the wisdom of the wise gals (the women in my family).

Is It a Sweet Potato or a Yam?

ALTHOUGH MANY PEOPLE use "sweet potato" and "yam" interchangeably, they are actually two very different vegetables. Sweet potatoes come in two varieties. The lighter sweet potato has a thinner, lighter skin and a pale-yellow flesh that is not terribly sweet, and has a texture similar to that of a white baking potato. The darker-skinned variety (which is most often called "yam" in error) has a thicker, dark-orange-to-reddish skin with a vivid orange, sweet flesh and a dense, moist texture.

By contrast, a true yam is the tuber of a tropical vine, and is not even distantly related to the sweet potato. Yams are more popular in Latin and Caribbean markets, and appear in more than 150 varieties around the world. Yams contain more natural sugar than sweet potatoes, and they have a higher moisture content. They are also marketed under their Spanish names, *boniato* and *ñame*.

Cane Syrup–Glazed Sweet Potatoes with Marshmallow Streusel

Pat: Gina's grandmother loved cane syrup, which is a sorghumlike syrup that has a deep bittersweet flavor. If you can't find cane syrup, use an equal amount of dark-brown sugar plus 2 tablespoons molasses. This dish gives a new twist to a classic Thanksgiving side. The gooey marshmallows and brown sugar keep the kids happy, while the "big kids" will love the addition of orange liqueur, warm spices, and pecans.

SWEET POTATOES

4 pounds dark-skinned sweet
    potatoes (see sidebar), peeled
    and cut into 1-inch cubes
1/3 cup cane syrup (see headnote)
5 tablespoons butter
1/2 teaspoon salt
2 teaspoons grated orange zest
2 tablespoons orange liqueur

STREUSEL TOPPING

1/2 cup butter, at room temperature
    and cut into pieces
1/2 cup light-brown sugar
1/2 cup all-purpose flour
1/4 teaspoon ground cinnamon
1/4 teaspoon salt
1 cup toasted pecan pieces
2 cups miniature marshmallows

Preheat the oven to 375°F.

Arrange the potatoes in 13 × 9 × 2-inch glass baking dish. Combine the cane syrup, butter, and salt in a small saucepan over medium heat. Bring to a boil, then remove the pan from the heat and stir in the orange zest and liqueur. Pour the sugar mixture over the potatoes, and toss the potatoes to coat. Cover the dish tightly with foil. Bake for 50 minutes, then remove the dish from the oven, take off the foil, and bake for another 20 minutes, until the potatoes are tender and the syrup has thickened slightly, basting occasionally.

Meanwhile, make the marshmallow streusel: Combine the butter, brown sugar, flour, cinnamon, salt, and pecans in the bowl of a food processor fitted with a metal blade, and pulse the mixture until it resembles coarse pebbles. Transfer the mixture to a bowl, then add the marshmallows and toss to combine.

Raise the oven temperature to 425°F. Top the sweet potatoes with the marshmallow streusel. Return to the oven, and bake until the topping is bubbly and browned, about 10 minutes.

SERVES 8

FIRST ROW: Gina's Grandma Mary, Ronnie's wife Judy, Gina's brother Ronnie, Gina's mom, and Gina at Ronnie's Ordination Service; Grandma Mary's eightieth birthday
SECOND ROW: The two queen bees in my life, Momma Lorine and Momma Jean
THIRD ROW: Gina's Grandma Mary
FOURTH ROW: Gina's mom at Shelbi's third birthday

Molasses-Baked Beans

Pat: All it takes is a spoon and a wedge of warm buttered cornbread to turn these sweet Southern baked beans, made with chunks of chopped pork, into a meal. Tangy baked beans are a Memphis trademark—we serve them sweeter than other regions around the country do. At our restaurants and at home, we flavor the beans with molasses, brown sugar, and our famous Neely's Barbecue Sauce—as well as plenty of chopped pork. The hickory flavor from chunks of smoked pork gives this dish some toothy tang.

---

1 tablespoon olive oil
¼ cup diced green bell pepper
¼ cup diced onion
One 48-ounce can baked beans
    (we like Allen's or Bush's)
¼ cup molasses
½ cup light-brown sugar
1 cup Neely's Barbecue Sauce
    (page 25)
⅓ cup Neely's Barbecue Seasoning
    (page 22)
½ cup chopped roast (or smoked)
    pork or beef

Preheat the oven to 275°F.

Heat the olive oil in a large skillet over medium-high heat. Add the bell pepper and onion, and sauté them until they soften, 4 to 5 minutes. Add the baked beans, molasses, brown sugar, Neely's Barbecue Sauce and Neely's Barbecue Seasoning to the skillet, and stir all the ingredients to combine. Transfer the bean mixture to a 9 × 13-inch baking pan. Add the meat, and stir well to combine. Cover the pan with aluminum foil, and bake for 45 minutes. Allow the beans to cool slightly, then serve warm, as a side dish.

SERVES 10 TO 12

Black-Eyed Peas with Bacon and Pork

Pat: Black-eyed peas, simmered with fatty pork (such as ham hocks or bacon), have been a staple in the South for hundreds of years. Inexpensive, easy to grow, and easy to store, they provide protein and nourishment and, many believe, good fortune (which is why eating black-eyed peas on New Year's Day is a Southern tradition). Some even eat greens, meant to symbolize money, alongside of them.

Don't worry if at the end of the cooking process these beans seem a little watery. To cream them up, mash the beans against the side of the pot with the back of a spoon, or purée a cup of them in the blender and add them back in. These black-eyed peas are great poured over warm cornbread, and are a perfect side with grilled or fried pork chops.

---

1 pound black-eyed peas (dried or fresh)
2 tablespoons vegetable oil
4 ounces pork shoulder, cut into ½-inch cubes
3 strips thick-sliced bacon, cut into ½-inch pieces
1 medium onion, diced small
4 garlic cloves, sliced
1½ teaspoons salt
1 teaspoon black pepper
½ teaspoon cayenne pepper
1 teaspoon garlic powder
4 cups Chicken Stock (page 28)
3 bay leaves
Hot-pepper vinegar, as desired

If using dried black-eyed peas, place them in a large pot and cover with about 4 inches of water. Soak the beans overnight, then drain and rinse. Alternatively, you can "quick-soak" the beans: bring them and the water to a boil for 2 minutes, then remove them from the heat, and cover the pot and soak for 1 hour. Drain and rinse the beans.

Heat the oil in a large pot over medium-high heat. When the oil is shimmering, add the pork. Cook until the pork is browned on all sides, 4 to 5 minutes. Add the bacon, onion, and garlic to the pot, and cook, stirring, for an additional 6 to 8 minutes, until the onion and garlic are lightly browned. Add the salt, black pepper, cayenne, and garlic powder, and cook for 2 more minutes, until the entire mixture is coated with spices. Add the stock, 2 cups water, and the bay leaves, bring the mixture to a boil, then reduce the heat and simmer, covered, for about 30 minutes.

When the pork begins to fall apart, add the soaked (or fresh) beans to the pot, and simmer for 1 to 1½ hours more, until the beans are very soft.

Using the back of a spoon, smash some of the beans against the inside of the pot, then stir into the mix. This will break up some beans and give them a creamier consistency. Alternatively, you can purée 1 cup of the beans and broth in a blender or a food processor, then return to the pot. Taste for seasonings, add hot-pepper vinegar, as desired, and serve.

SERVES 6 TO 8

Glazed Autumn Root Vegetables

Gina: This simple, beautiful braise of sweet root vegetables and shallots is a perfect complement to any roasted meat (a Thanksgiving turkey, Cornish hens, and pot roast come to mind). For the deepest, richest flavor, be sure to get a good brown color on the vegetables before adding them to the chicken stock. We finish the dish with sage and parsley, but any number of fresh herbs will do the trick, including rosemary, thyme, or oregano.

---

2 tablespoons butter

1 tablespoon olive oil

1 large (1-pound) rutabaga, peeled, cut into 1-inch cubes

1 pound turnips, peeled, cut into 1-inch cubes

1 pound carrots, peeled, cut into 1-inch cubes

4 large shallots, peeled and halved

Kosher salt

Freshly ground black pepper

1 cup Chicken Stock (page 28)

2 tablespoons honey

2 tablespoons apple-cider vinegar

2 tablespoons chopped fresh sage leaves

2 tablespoons chopped fresh flat-leaf parsley

Melt the butter with the olive oil in a large skillet over high heat. Add the rutabaga, turnips, carrots, and shallots, season with salt and pepper, and sauté until they are browned on all sides, about 8 minutes total. Add the stock to the skillet and cover, reduce the heat to low, and then simmer the vegetables until they are tender, stirring occasionally, about 10 minutes. Uncover the skillet, increase the heat to high, and bring the liquid to a boil. Stir in the honey, vinegar, sage, and parsley, and cook until the sauce is reduced to a glaze, stirring often, 3 to 4 minutes. Taste for seasonings, and add more salt and pepper, as desired.

SERVES 6 TO 8

Dig In: Savory, Soulful Entrées

Pat: Of all the chapters in our book, this one feels the most personal, because the recipes collected here read like a time line of my life. The hearty comfort foods that my momma prepared while we were growing up—pot roast with carrots and potatoes, fried pork chops simmered in a homemade vegetable soup, lasagna—bring back memories of sitting around the family table and the gratitude we all felt for having been fed a nourishing meal. When I was a boy, coming home after school or football practice, Momma's cooking provided great comfort. It said to me—and to my siblings—that someone cared.

Then, of course, there is barbecue. Our award-winning smoked pork and beef ribs, barbecued chicken, and tender rib tips conjure up not only the business we are still running but the years Tony and I spent learning our trade. I can't tell you how many hours and hours we spent sweating it out over hickory pits. Sometimes I think it was all that smoke that provided the inspiration for some of our signature menu items (such as Barbecue Spaghetti). Or maybe we're just crazy.

Finally, there are the recipes we prepare at home. Like most parents, Gina and I are busy with work, schedules (our gals' and our own), and everything else. It's often a struggle to get a home-cooked meal on the table (especially these days, when we are spending much of our time living out of a suitcase!). Still, we find a way to do it. Not every day, mind you, but we're in the kitchen cooking with our gals at least once a week. And you should be, too. Gina and I feel **nothing is more important than sharing a meal with your family**. It's just another example of how like-minded we are.

Of course, the meals we are cooking these days are ones that are most familiar. They're dishes that our moms cooked for us. And we wouldn't have it any other way. After all, our mothers couldn't afford to treat their families to restaurant meals or takeout. So our palates became accustomed to great home cooking. Now our daughters, Spenser and Shelbi, are enjoying some of the same dishes we enjoyed as kids. And even though times are better for us financially, why would we want to deny our kids the great traditions that served us both so well?

Gina and Pat dig into super-stuffed taters; mini loaf pans make nifty serving containers.

Barbecue Baked Potatoes

Pat: Brushed with butter, rubbed with spices, and dressed the way you want it, our barbecue baked potatoes (which are essentially baked potatoes loaded with toppings) will make your stomach skip a beat. These are fun to make with your kids, because they can dress up their taters with all kinds of goodness—meat, sour cream, shredded cheese, chives, and so forth. Depending on what stuff and how much of it you load onto each potato, these can serve as a side dish or an entire meal. For a healthier spud, Gina follows this recipe with a lightened-up twice-baked tater that is just as tasty as my belt-busting variety.

---

2 extra-large baking potatoes

2 tablespoons butter, melted, plus more for garnish

¼ teaspoon Neely's Barbecue Seasoning (page 22)

½ cup chopped cooked pork or beef (e.g., roasted or barbecued meat, or browned ground meat)

¼ cup Neely's Barbecue Sauce (page 25)

4 tablespoons shredded cheddar cheese, for garnish

Sour cream, for garnish

Chives (dried or snipped fresh), for garnish

Preheat the oven to 425°F.

Scrub the potatoes under warm water, then prick them with a fork. Brush them with the melted butter, then sprinkle them with Neely's Barbecue Seasoning, place them on a baking sheet, and bake for 1 hour, until they are soft but not overcooked. Let the potatoes cool for about 15 minutes (until they are cool enough to handle), and then cut them in half lengthwise.

Heat the meat and Neely's Barbecue Sauce in a small saucepan or in the microwave until warmed through. Top the potato halves with a ¼ cup of the barbecued meat, and garnish with additional butter, cheddar cheese, sour cream, and chives, as desired.

MAKES 2 STUFFED POTATOES, SERVING 2 TO 4

Gina's "Skinny Jeans" Potatoes

2 extra-large baking potatoes
1 teaspoon vegetable oil
¼ teaspoon Neely's Barbecue
    Seasoning (page 22)
2 tablespoons butter
¼ cup buttermilk
2 ounces Neufchâtel (reduced-fat
    cream cheese)
2 scallions, finely chopped
Kosher salt
Freshly ground black pepper
Dash hot sauce
½ cup chopped roasted or smoked
    turkey or chicken
¼ cup Neely's Barbecue Sauce
    (page 25)
Shredded cheddar cheese, for
    garnish
Snipped fresh chives, for garnish

Preheat the oven to 425°F.

Scrub the potatoes well under warm water, then rub them with the oil and Neely's Barbecue Seasoning. Place them on a baking sheet or directly on the baking rack of your oven, and bake them for 1 hour, or until they are tender but not over-cooked. Let the potatoes cool for about 15 minutes, or until they are cool enough to handle, and then cut them in half length-wise. Using a spoon, scoop out most of the potato meat and put it into a mixing bowl (reserve enough of the potato to form a sturdy shell).

Add the butter, buttermilk, Neufchâtel, scallions, salt and pepper to taste, and the hot sauce to the bowl with the pota-toes, and stir everything gently with a whisk until the butter melts into the mixture. Add the turkey or chicken and Neely's Barbecue Sauce, and mix together. I like my tater stuffing on the rustic side, so it doesn't have to be perfectly smooth. Use a spoon to place the stuffing back into the potato shell (if you want to get fancy, you can also use a pastry bag with a large hole and pipe the mixture back into the potato shell). Garnish with cheddar cheese, then return the stuffed potatoes to the oven and bake for another 15 to 20 minutes, until the tops are very lightly browned. Garnish the baked potatoes with the snipped chives, and serve.

MAKES 2 STUFFED POTATOES, SERVING 2 TO 4

Barbecue Spaghetti

Pat: A passion for pasta via Memphis equals . . . barbecue spaghetti?!? Initially, our customers were skeptical about trying this dish—that is, until Tony and I started giving out free samples to everyone who came through the door. After about two weeks, the sampling wasn't necessary, because people were hooked. These days we go through about 200 gallons of barbecue spaghetti a week; people from all over the country go wild for the tangy, saucy noodles tossed with smoky chunks of meat (it's become one of our best-selling dishes). And we promise, after making this dish, you'll understand why. Serve it as a side dish (with barbecued or roasted meats) or as a meal.

2 tablespoons olive oil
¼ cup diced yellow onion
½ cup diced green bell pepper
2 garlic cloves, minced
4 cups Neely's Barbecue Sauce
    (page 25)
2 pounds cooked spaghetti
2 pounds smoked pork, beef,
    or chicken, coarsely chopped
    (see note)
Hot sauce (optional)

NOTE: You can also use grilled or roasted meat, although it won't deliver the same smoky flavor.

Heat the olive oil in a large skillet over medium heat. Add the onion, bell pepper, and garlic, and cook, stirring frequently to prevent from sticking, until the vegetables have softened, 3 to 4 minutes. Reduce the heat to low, stir in the Neely's Barbecue Sauce, and simmer for about 5 minutes, until slightly reduced. When you're ready to serve the dish, add the spaghetti, smoked meat, and hot sauce, if desired, and toss well to combine.

SERVES 8 TO 10

Barbecue Pizza with Onions and Peppers

Pat: If you haven't figured this out by now, in Memphis we find a way to barbecue everything. One day Tony and I turned our attention to flatbread and—surprise, surprise—we came up with a recipe for barbecue pizza! We make ours with a crispy grilled crust, sautéed onions and peppers, and barbecue sauce, and then top the whole thing with one of our favorite cooked meats. It's a Neely game-time staple, because the dough and toppings can be made hours in advance, so the pizzas can be assembled in minutes and popped into the oven.

Don't be intimidated by the crust—our homemade dough is easy to make and a great project to work on with your kids. In our house, it's not a pizza party until everyone is dusted with flour.

PIZZA DOUGH

1 package active dry yeast

1½ cups warm water (105 to 115°F)

1 teaspoon honey

3 tablespoons olive oil, plus more for greasing

1 tablespoon kosher salt

3½ cups bread flour

PIZZA

2 tablespoons olive oil

1 small onion, thinly sliced

½ green bell pepper, thinly sliced

2 garlic cloves, thinly sliced

1 cup Neely's Barbecue Sauce (page 25)

2 cups chopped cooked pork, beef, or chicken

One 8-ounce package shredded mozzarella

¼ cup grated Parmesan cheese

Place the yeast, warm water, and honey in a small bowl, and stir to dissolve. When the yeast mixture is foamy, stir in the olive oil and salt.

Place the flour and the yeast mixture in the bowl of an electric mixer. Using the dough hook, mix at low speed for about 8 minutes, then increase the speed to medium and knead until the dough is elastic and starting to pull away from the sides of the bowl, about 3 minutes. The dough should be smooth and firm. Ball up the dough, and place it in a large, well-oiled glass bowl. Flip the dough ball to coat both sides with oil. Cover with plastic wrap, and let rise in a warm, draft-free area for 2 hours, until doubled in bulk.

Lightly flour a large cutting board or baking sheet. Divide the dough into four equal pieces, shape each into a ball, and allow the pieces to rest for 20 more minutes before cooking.

When you're ready to cook the pizza, preheat the grill to high and the oven to 425°F.

Heat 1 tablespoon of the olive oil in a medium skillet over medium heat. Add the onion, bell pepper, and garlic, and sauté until tender, about 5 minutes. Transfer to a glass bowl.

Lightly flour a work surface, and roll out the four balls of dough into 6-inch circles that are ¼ to ⅛ inch thick. Brush each round of dough with the remaining tablespoon of olive oil, and place on grill. Grill for 2 to 3 minutes on the first side. Flip, and cook for 1 more minute. Transfer the grilled crusts to a sheet tray, and repeat with the other dough balls.

To assemble the pizzas, spread ¼ cup of barbecue sauce evenly on each pizza, then top with ½ cup of chopped meat and a quarter of the sautéed vegetables. Sprinkle each pizza with a handful of mozzarella and a few pinches of grated Parmesan. Bake the pizzas for 10 minutes, or until the cheese is melted. Serve immediately.

SERVES 4

NOTE: If you don't want to pregrill the crusts, simply top the dough with the toppings as described above and bake for an additional 6 to 8 minutes, or until the dough is crisp and the cheese is bubbly and melted. You'll lose that char-grilled goodness, but your final results will be just as crisp.

Working in the restaurant is as much fun as hanging out at home.
FIRST ROW: Gina at work; Neely brothers
SECOND ROW: Gaelin, Spenser, Pat, and Mark; Tony giving his son Little Tony Jr. a lesson at the grill
THIRD ROW: Chef Pat Neely

Lorine's Lasagna

Pat: This is another one of those dishes that take me back to my childhood. I loved my momma Lorine's lasagna, and to this day, I crave the molten layers of gooey cheese, rich tomato sauce, tender noodles, and beef. The pleasure of this dish is not just in the eating, it's in the making and baking. When Momma's lasagna is in the oven, our entire house smells like an Italian grandma has moved in. Lucky for me, my family loves this dish as much as I do, and Gina has learned to make this lasagna as well as my mom does. We like to make ours with cottage cheese, because we love the tangy flavor, but you can substitute the traditional ricotta if you prefer.

---

1 tablespoon olive oil, plus more for greasing
1 pound ground beef (not lean)
1 medium onion, chopped
2 garlic cloves, minced
One 28-ounce can crushed tomatoes
One 6-ounce can tomato paste
1 teaspoon dried oregano
Kosher salt
Freshly ground black pepper
2 large eggs
2 cups small curd cottage cheese or ricotta
¾ cup grated Parmesan cheese
1 tablespoon chopped fresh flat-leaf parsley
Two 8-ounce bags shredded mozzarella cheese
One 8-ounce bag shredded cheddar cheese
One 8-ounce box "no boil" lasagna noodles (you should have 12 noodles)

Preheat the oven to 375°F. Brush a small amount of olive oil over the bottom and sides of a 13 × 9 × 2-inch baking dish.

Heat the oil in a large sauté pan over medium-high heat. Add the ground beef, onion, and garlic, and sauté, breaking up the beef with a wooden spoon, until the meat is browned. Add the tomatoes, tomato paste, and oregano. Cover, reduce the heat to medium-low, and simmer for 15 minutes, stirring occasionally. Season to taste with salt and pepper.

In a large bowl, whisk the eggs together, then stir in the cottage cheese, ½ cup of the Parmesan, the parsley, 1 teaspoon salt, and ½ teaspoon black pepper. Combine the mozzarella and cheddar cheeses in a bowl. Spread 1 cup of the meat sauce over the bottom of the prepared baking dish. Lay four noodles over the sauce, overlapping if necessary. Spread half of the cottage cheese mixture over top. Sprinkle 1¾ cups of the mozzarella-cheddar mixture over the cottage cheese mixture. Ladle 1¾ cups of the meat sauce over the cheese. Repeat layering in the same order (noodles, cottage cheese, etc.). Finish with the remaining four noodles, and top with ½ cup sauce and ½ cup mozzarella and cheddar. Top with the remaining ¼ cup Parmesan.

Cover the pan with foil and bake in center of oven for 30 minutes. Uncover the pan and bake for about another 10 minutes, until the sauce is bubbling around the edges. Let the lasagna stand for 10 minutes before serving.

SERVES 6 TO 8

Grilled Shrimp Pasta with Tomatoes, Black Olives, and Feta

Gina: If you've never spent a summer in the South, then you don't know heat like *we* know heat! Baby, this dish is perfect for a sultry Memphis evening, because it requires very little cooking. The shrimp and zucchini are grilled briefly, and the rest of the ingredients are simply heated in olive oil for a few minutes, to coax out their flavor. Then everything is tossed with pasta shells, and you are done, sugar. We call for cherry tomatoes, but feel free to use Sweet 100, currant, or pear tomatoes, or any other small tomatoes available at your local farmers' market. Best of all, you'll walk away from the table feeling satisfied but not too full. Choose a nice Chardonnay or Pinot Grigio, and you are set.

½ cup olive oil, plus more for brushing shrimp
1 pint cherry tomatoes, halved
2 garlic cloves, thinly sliced
¼ teaspoon crushed red-pepper flakes
3 tablespoons red-wine vinegar
Kosher salt
1 pound medium shrimp, peeled and deveined
Freshly ground black pepper
2 small zucchini, cut lengthwise into ½-inch-thick slices
1 pound pasta shells
3 scallions, thinly sliced
⅓ cup coarsely chopped oil-cured black olives
2 teaspoons lemon zest
2 tablespoons chopped fresh mint or flat-leaf parsley leaves
6 ounces feta cheese, crumbled

Heat the olive oil, tomatoes, garlic, red-pepper flakes, vinegar, and a pinch of salt in a large, deep skillet over medium heat until just warmed through (the tomatoes will begin to soften and release their juice). Remove from the heat, and set aside to marinate.

Heat the grill to medium-high. Bring a large pot of lightly salted water to a boil.

Thread the shrimp onto skewers, brush with olive oil, and sprinkle with salt and pepper. Brush the zucchini slices with olive oil, and season with salt and pepper. Grill the shrimp until just opaque throughout, 2 to 3 minutes per side. Grill the zucchini for 2 to 3 minutes on each side, until they are just tender and nice grill marks appear. Remove the shrimp from the skewers, and coarsely chop. Cut the zucchini into ½-inch pieces. Toss the shrimp and zucchini in a medium bowl, and set aside.

Cook the pasta until just tender, about 8 minutes. Drain but do not rinse. Transfer the pasta to a large mixing bowl, pour in the tomato mixture, and toss well to combine. Add the shrimp and zucchini and toss; add the scallions, olives, lemon zest, mint (or parsley), and half of the feta, and toss well to combine. Taste for seasonings, and add more salt or pepper as desired. Transfer to a large serving bowl, and top with the remaining feta.

SERVES 4 TO 6

Spicy Salmon with Mustard and Brown Sugar Glaze

Gina: It's happening to all of us: *we're getting older.* That's the bad news. The good news is that there are foods we can eat that have indisputable heath benefits, and salmon is one of them. That wouldn't excite me nearly as much if the fish wasn't so sweet and delicious. Pat and I were on board with salmon from the get-go, but trying to introduce it to our girls was a challenge. I thought if I added just a hint of sweetness I could ease it on them. So I created this sweet and spicy sauce using mustard and brown sugar. Score one for Mom! The sauce caramelizes under the broiler, and the resulting glaze is a perfect complement to the rich-tasting salmon.

If you didn't already know it, I am the baby sister in my family, in every sense of the word. My older sisters think it's ironic when I cook for them, because they all spoiled me so much when I was growing up (now Pat continues that tradition, and it all works for me). My big sister Tanya—she's the more athletic one, who's always telling me to hold my stomach in and keep my back straight—actually viewed me differently once I made this dish.

We like to splurge on wild salmon, because it's the absolute best for you, and the flavor is as sweet as candy.

---

1 cup dry white wine
2 tablespoons butter
1 teaspoon Old Bay Seasoning
2 teaspoons drained capers
Pinch cayenne pepper
One 2-pound center-cut wild
    salmon fillet, skin removed
Kosher salt
Freshly ground black pepper
⅓ cup spicy brown mustard
¼ cup firmly packed light-brown
    sugar

Preheat the oven to 300°F. Heat the wine, butter, Old Bay Seasoning, capers, and cayenne in a small saucepan over medium-high heat. Bring the mixture to a boil, reduce the heat to low, and simmer for 3 to 4 minutes.

Sprinkle the salmon on both sides with salt and pepper. Place the fish in a glass baking dish. Pour the wine mixture over the top, and bake until fish is opaque in the center, 15 to 17 minutes; remove from the oven.

Preheat the broiler. Whisk together the mustard and sugar in a small bowl; spread over the salmon to cover. Broil the salmon until the topping is brown and bubbling, about 3 minutes. Transfer the salmon to a platter and serve.

SERVES 6

Grilled Halibut and Asparagus with Barbecue Butter

Gina: This is an idea that Pat and I hatched when we were thinking of other ways to use our Neely's Barbecue Seasoning. We were already sprinkling it over various meats, and I was using it to season catfish. So, one evening when I was having a cocktail (which is when I am most creative), I thought, why not combine the barbecue seasoning with butter?!? I checked with Pat, and he thought it was a great idea, and, voilà, barbecue butter was born. You know, some of our best dishes have come from just messing around, so you might want to do what we do and let yourself go in the kitchen!

During warm weather, when we don't have the time (or the desire) to stand over a hot stove, few meals are as enticing as a piece of grilled fish like halibut, tuna, or salmon alongside grilled spears of asparagus slathered with this lively butter. The addictive butter (flavored with fresh herbs, scallions, and orange zest) is also incredibly versatile. Try it tossed with pasta and grilled shrimp, or melted over a seared steak. Boiled creamy new potatoes or steamed rice is a great accompaniment to this simple, satisfying meal.

Barbecue butter will keep in the fridge for 4 or 5 days.

---

1 teaspoon finely chopped fresh
    oregano leaves
1 scallion, white and light-green
    parts, finely chopped
6 tablespoons butter, at room
    temperature
2 teaspoons Neely's Barbecue
    Seasoning (page 22)
1 teaspoon grated orange zest
Kosher salt
Pinch cayenne pepper
Six 6-ounce halibut fillets, about
    1 inch thick
Extra-virgin olive oil, for brushing
    fish and asparagus
Freshly ground black pepper
2 pounds asparagus, trimmed

Using a rubber spatula, combine the oregano, scallion, butter, Neely's Barbecue Seasoning, orange zest, $\frac{1}{4}$ teaspoon salt, and cayenne. Transfer the seasoned butter onto a piece of plastic wrap. Using the plastic wrap as a shield for your hands, shape the butter into a log, wrap with the plastic wrap, and chill for at least 30 minutes.

Heat the grill to medium-high. Brush the fish fillets on both sides with olive oil, and season with salt and freshly ground black pepper; set aside.

Brush the asparagus with oil and season with salt and black pepper. Grill the spears until they are tender, turning them once, about 6 minutes total.

Grill the halibut fillets about 4 minutes per side, until the center of the fish is opaque and firm. Transfer the fish and asparagus to plates. Spread a generous tablespoon of the barbecue butter over the fish. Serve, passing additional barbecue butter alongside.

SERVES 6

Chicken with Creole Mustard Cream Sauce

Gina: This dish is a Southerner's take on the classic French-style sauté of chicken, shallots, cream, and tarragon—a killer combination of flavors. Give this recipe to anyone who claims they don't have time to make dinner, because it comes together in minutes, and the results are just as good as—or better than—anything you can order at a restaurant. I like to serve this dish with white rice to soak up the cream sauce, some steamed green beans with butter, and a crisp white wine.

I remember complaining about being served chicken when I was a little girl, and my mother telling me, "Chicken is the house steak." She was right! My mother could work a chicken over, from grilling, boiling, frying, baking, and so on—she served it so many ways that I thought she was a magician. Well, you know the old adage that you become your mother? Spenser asked me the same question the other night ("Chicken again?"), and I couldn't do anything but respond, "Chicken is the house steak." We both laughed, and all those memories came flooding back to me. I loved it!

---

6 large boneless, skinless chicken
    breast halves, trimmed
Kosher salt
Freshly ground black pepper
½ cup plus 1 teaspoon all-purpose
    flour
2 tablespoons olive oil
1 tablespoon butter
1 cup Chicken Stock (page 28),
    plus more as needed
2 large shallots, finely chopped
½ cup white wine
½ cup heavy cream
Juice of 1 lemon
2 tablespoons Creole mustard
    (see page 93)
3 tablespoons finely minced fresh
    tarragon leaves, plus sprigs for
    garnish

Rinse the chicken, pat dry with paper towels, and season with salt and pepper. Place the flour in a pie tin and dredge the chicken breasts lightly in the flour, shaking off any excess. Discard leftover flour.

Heat the olive oil and butter in a large skillet over medium-high heat. Sauté the chicken, turning once, until nicely browned on both sides, about 10 minutes total. Add ½ cup of the stock, reduce the heat, cover, and simmer until the chicken is cooked through, 4 to 6 minutes. (Check to make sure the pan juices don't run dry. If necessary, add a bit of stock to prevent scorching.) Transfer the chicken to a plate, and tent with foil.

Add the shallots to the skillet, and cook, stirring, until softened. Add the wine, bring to a boil, and cook until reduced to about ¼ cup, 2 to 4 minutes. Reduce the heat to low, then whisk in the cream, lemon juice, and mustard, and simmer until the sauce coats a spoon, 1 to 2 minutes.

Return the chicken to the pan along with the minced tarragon. Turn to coat with the sauce, and cook until heated through, 1 to 2 minutes. Serve the chicken over rice, drizzling the remaining sauce over the top. Garnish with sprigs of tarragon.

SERVES 6

Wet and Dry Chicken

Pat: In Memphis, barbecued meats are ordered either "dry" or "wet." "Dry" meats are coated with a dry spice rub before they're cooked, and often sprinkled with those seasonings when they come off the grill. "Wet" meats are slathered with barbecue sauce. Folks who crave a double dose of flavor, like me, order foods "wet and dry," meaning that the meat is sprinkled with dry rub before being cooked, then slathered with sauce afterward.

This Memphis pit tradition has found its way into the repertoire of home cooks as well. The application of a dry rub works for meats cooked on the grill or, as our mothers are fond of doing, in the oven. In this recipe, we douse our chicken with a dry rub and then bake it in barbecue sauce. The result is moist, flavorful, falling-off-the-bone tender chicken. We serve this saucy chicken with steamed rice or hot buttered rolls to soak up all the tomatoey goodness, and the accompanying vegetables on the side. It's no wonder the Neely boys became so good with the grill when Momma was feeding us dishes like this from her kitchen oven.

---

6 bone-in chicken-breast halves, or
   12 bone-in chicken thighs
2 tablespoons Neely's Barbecue
   Seasoning (page 22)
Kosher salt
Freshly ground black pepper
2 tablespoons vegetable oil
2 large onions, thinly sliced
2 celery stalks, finely chopped
1 large carrot, finely chopped
2 cups Neely's Barbecue Sauce
   (page 25)
½ cup Chicken Stock (page 28)

Place the chicken in a 9 × 13-inch baking dish and sprinkle with Neely's Barbecue Seasoning and a generous amount of salt and pepper. Allow the chicken to marinate for at least 1 hour in the fridge, or, better yet, overnight.

Preheat the oven to 325°F.

Allow the chicken to come to room temperature. Heat the oil in a large skillet over medium-high heat. Add the onions, celery, carrot, and a pinch of salt and pepper, and cook, stirring, until the vegetables have softened, about 7 minutes. Stir in the Neely's Barbecue Sauce and the stock. Cool slightly, then pour the vegetable mixture over the chicken breasts, tossing the chicken to coat. Bake the chicken until cooked through and tender, about 30 minutes for breasts and 40 to 45 minutes for thighs. Serve immediately with hot steamed rice or buttered rolls, and steamed broccoli, if desired.

SERVES 6

Spicy Fried Chicken

Pat: When I was growing up in the South, there were "soul food" restaurants on every corner. I mean *every* corner. And there was one entrée served in all those restaurants, and that, of course, was fried chicken.

Gina: To this day, in spite of our occasional diets, fried chicken is one menu item that is hard to resist. It has been and always will be one of our weaknesses. But it's one we can live with.

When you've had a bad day at work, there's something about coming home to a good piece of fried chicken. It's a Southern tonic: a feel-good, make-it-all-better food.

Pat: We coat the chicken in dry spices first. This allows an incredible flavor to penetrate and permeate the meat. Then the chicken is double-dipped in buttermilk and seasoned flour to create a crispy, flavorful crunch. I promise you lip-smackin' good fried chicken with this Neely favorite. It's one of those dishes that partygoers love and are still talking about the next day.

Two 3- to 4-pound chickens, each
    cut into 8 pieces
3 tablespoons hot sauce
¼ cup Neely's Barbecue Seasoning
    (page 22)
1¼ teaspoons salt
1 teaspoon freshly ground black
    pepper
½ teaspoon cayenne pepper
¼ teaspoon white pepper
½ teaspoon garlic powder
2 cups well-shaken buttermilk
4 cups all-purpose flour
Peanut oil, for frying

Place the chicken pieces in a large bowl. Pour the hot sauce over the chicken. In a small bowl, whisk together 2 tablespoons of the Neely's Barbecue Seasoning with the salt, black pepper, cayenne, white pepper, and garlic powder. Add the spice mixture to the chicken and massage all the ingredients into the pieces with your hands. Cover the chicken with plastic wrap and marinate for at least 1 hour, or for up to 1 day in the refrigerator (the longer the better, to allow the seasonings to permeate the chicken).

Pour the buttermilk over the chicken pieces and toss to coat. Pour the flour into a large bowl.

Heat the oil in a Dutch oven or a large cast-iron skillet to 350°F, or until a pinch of flour sizzles when it is dropped in the fat. As the oil heats, remove the chicken pieces from the buttermilk, allowing the excess buttermilk to drip off.

Transfer the chicken, several pieces at a time, to the bowl with the flour. Toss to coat. Remove the chicken pieces from the flour, shaking off any excess, and place the chicken, one piece at a time, in the Dutch oven. Fry the chicken in several batches. For the crispiest results, do not overcrowd the Dutch oven. One of the secrets to deep-frying is maintaining a constant cooking temperature (the oil in the oven or skillet should be somewhat lively, having a mellow sizzle but not a raging boil). Fry the chicken for 16 to 18 minutes, using tongs as necessary to turn the pieces. When the chicken bobs, it's done. That's right (another Neely secret): your chicken will float to the top of the Dutch oven when she's done!

SERVES 4 TO 6

NOTE: Remember how your mom used to tell you to wash your hands before supper? She was right! Anytime you are working with food—especially meat, poultry, or seafood—you need to wash your hands before and after handling the food. And you really need to scrub all of your work surfaces and kitchen utensils, as well. The clean hands rule certainly applies to this dish, because I guarantee that when you plate up the fried chicken and start eating, you will not be able to resist licking your fingers (it's that good). At the Neelys', some of our dishes are so messy we wash our hands after supper as well.

One of my favorite meals to make at home is fried chicken.

When a pinch of flour sizzles in the hot oil, you're ready to cook. For the crispiest results, don't over-crowd the pan. When the chicken floats or bobs in the oil, it's done. Drain the fried pieces on paper towels and you've got a finger-lickin' platter from heaven!

Spiced Cornish Hens with Cornbread and Sausage Stuffing

Gina: Pat and I love, absolutely love, Cornish hens. One year we took a family vacation to Florida's Gulf Shore for Thanksgiving. When we got there, we had a beach view as well as the beach to ourselves. It was going to be a *special* Thanksgiving.

Here's what happened: Before we left for our vacation, Pat begged me not to go overboard packing the foodstuffs. He said, "I don't want to smell collard greens up the road." Well, I said, "Too bad," because I knew stores might not be open, and I needed my ingredients for cooking the birds. See, ladies, this is why we are so special, because we *know*. Well, guess what, when we got to the coast, we couldn't find any stores that were open. So it was lucky for us that a smart momma had packed all her ingredients, and we were able to cook our entire Thanksgiving dinner. Long story short: It was a wonderful meal. We enjoyed our dinner overlooking a beautiful beach, and the meal remains one of our most cherished memories. Lesson here, ladies: Never let a man tell you what to pack!

As for the birds, they are surprisingly easy to prepare. After the hens are rubbed with spices, the fragrant cornbread stuffing can be assembled in minutes in one skillet. The real appeal is the flavor and the stylish presentation. This recipe promises to be a holiday staple for years to come, with or without the view!

2 teaspoons salt

2 teaspoon ground cumin

1 teaspoon pure ground chile
     powder

1 teaspoon freshly ground
     black pepper

½ teaspoon ground allspice

4 Cornish game hens, halved
     lengthwise

2 teaspoons Dijon mustard

**CORNBREAD-AND-SAUSAGE
     STUFFING**

12 ounces ground pork sausage

2 tablespoons vegetable or olive oil,
     plus more for greasing

1 medium onion, chopped

⅓ cup chopped celery

1 jalapeño, seeded and minced

1 teaspoon chopped fresh thyme
     leaves (or ½ teaspoon dried
     thyme)

4 cups crumbled cornbread

½ cup Chicken Stock (page 28)
     or low-sodium canned broth

2 tablespoons chopped fresh
     flat-leaf parsley

2 tablespoons chopped fresh
     cilantro leaves and tender stems
     (optional)

Kosher salt

Freshly ground black pepper

Whisk together the dry ingredients—the salt, cumin, chile powder, black pepper, and allspice—in a small bowl. Season both sides of the hens with this mix, and set them aside to marinate for 30 minutes at room temperature or for up to 8 hours in the refrigerator. Meanwhile, prepare the stuffing.

Cook the sausage in a large, heavy skillet over medium heat until no pink remains, about 8 minutes. Using a slotted spoon, transfer the sausage to a plate lined with paper towels; drain all but 1 tablespoon of fat from the skillet. Return the skillet to the heat, and add the oil. Add the onion, celery, and jalapeño, and cook, stirring, until the vegetables have softened, about 6 minutes. Stir in the thyme, crumbled cornbread, sausage, chicken stock, parsley, and cilantro, if desired. Remove the skillet from the heat; taste the stuffing for seasoning, and add salt and pepper as desired.

Preheat the oven to 375°F. Grease two 13 × 9 × 2-inch baking dishes with oil.

Place the hens skin-side down on a work surface. Pack one-fourth of the stuffing into each cavity. Arrange the hens stuffing-side down in the prepared dish. Brush the tops of the hens with the mustard. Roast the hens until they are golden brown and juices run clear when thighs are pierced, 50 to 55 minutes. Transfer the hens to a platter, and serve.

SERVES 4

Aunt Faye's Chicken with Scallion Dumplings

Gina: Ladies! The things we go through to please our men! You should be fully aware that Aunt Faye is Pat's favorite aunt, so you know I had to get this recipe down right.

Pat: My dear and favorite aunt, Faye, is my late father's oldest sister. She lives in Chicago, and for a while, when we were children, we lived there, too. During those years, Aunt Faye would cook us chicken and dumplings. Needless to say, it became one of my favorite dishes (and the fact that my favorite aunt was preparing it made it all the better!).

CHICKEN
2 tablespoons olive oil
4 whole leg-thigh chicken pieces
Kosher salt
Freshly ground black pepper
1 onion, quartered
2 whole cloves
3 cups Chicken Stock (page 28)
2 sprigs fresh thyme (optional)

STEW
2 tablespoons olive oil
1 tablespoon butter
2 leeks, white and pale green parts
   only, thinly sliced
2 celery stalks, thinly sliced
2 garlic cloves, minced
1 teaspoon chopped fresh thyme
   leaves
1 teaspoon chopped fresh sage
   leaves
3 tablespoons all-purpose flour
1 cup half-and-half
4 cups Chicken Stock (page 28)
2 medium turnips, peeled and diced
1 cup diced carrots
1 cup frozen peas
Kosher salt
Freshly ground black pepper
1 recipe Scallion Dumplings
   (recipe follows)

To make the chicken, heat the olive oil in a large sauté pan or Dutch oven over medium-high heat. Season the chicken generously with salt and pepper. When the oil is very hot, add the chicken, and cook, turning once, until it is well browned on both sides, about 10 minutes total. Pour off the excess oil, and add the stock, the onion pierced with the two cloves (so that two quarters have one clove each), and the thyme sprigs, if desired. Add enough water just to cover the chicken, and bring to a boil. Reduce the heat to low, and simmer, covered, until the meat is tender and coming away from the bone, 40 to 50 minutes. (Alternatively, this can be cooked, covered, in a 250°F oven.)

Remove from the heat, allow the chicken to cool, and drain, reserving liquid (you should have 3 to 4 cups). When the chicken is cool enough to handle, pick the meat off the bones and set aside; discard the bones.

Preheat the oven to 400°F.

To make the stew, in a heavy ovenproof pot or Dutch oven, heat the olive oil and butter over medium heat. Add the leeks and celery, and sauté until leeks are tender, about 5 minutes. Add the garlic, thyme, and sage, and sauté for another minute. Sprinkle in the flour, and cook, stirring, for 2 to 3 minutes, until the vegetables are well coated. Whisk in the half-and-half and 1 cup of the stock and bring to a boil. Whisk in the remaining 3 cups of stock (if you have less, make up the difference with water), then add the turnips and carrots. Return to a boil, reduce the heat to low, then add the chicken meat and a pinch of salt, and simmer gently, stirring from time to time, for about

15 minutes, until the carrots and turnips are tender. Taste for seasonings, and add more salt and freshly ground black pepper as desired. Stir in the peas. Mix up the dumpling dough and drop heaping tablespoons of the dough onto the surface of the stew. Place, uncovered, in the oven and bake for 12 to 15 minutes, until the surface of the dumplings is dry to the touch and golden brown.

SERVES 6

Scallion Dumplings

1½ cups all-purpose flour
½ cup cornmeal
2 teaspoons baking powder
¾ teaspoon salt
Pinch cayenne pepper
Freshly ground black pepper
1 large egg, beaten with a fork
⅔ cup milk
2 tablespoons butter, melted
4 scallions, finely chopped

In a small bowl, whisk together the flour, cornmeal, baking powder, salt, cayenne, and a generous grinding of black pepper. In another bowl, use a fork to stir together the egg, milk, butter, and scallions. Stir the dry ingredients into the wet ingredients to make a stiff batter; season with a generous grinding of black pepper.

Aunt Faye

Over the years, Gina and I have always
travel, dine, and spend exciting times to
FIRST ROW: Pat and Gina in Mexico; Pat a
at the restaurant at their ten-year hig
reunion
SECOND ROW: Pat and Gina stylin'; Pat an
at her Miss Congeniality coronation
THIRD ROW: Pat and Gina on a cruise shi
can't see the drinks in our hands)

Barbecue Turkey Meatloaf

Gina: This recipe came from my *fabulous* "girlfriend" D'Won (every girl needs a D'Won in her circle). D'Won is a huge turkey-lover, an amateur chef, and the best personal shopper around. When I was visiting him in Atlanta, we cooked up this recipe and it was spot-on. It's essentially a red dress for the meatloaf (and y'all know everything looks and tastes better in a red dress!).

Pat: This is one of those dishes where we splash on barbecue sauce without firing up the grill. During the early days of our post-reunion courtship, Gina would prepare this delicious meatloaf for me. She replaced ketchup, traditionally used in meatloaf recipes, with Neely's Barbecue Sauce and Seasoning. Looking back on it, I think that just might have sealed the deal. I remember thinking at the time that any woman who can light a fire under a red-meat man with a turkey loaf—well, that woman is *special.*

Gina: This meatloaf is so full of flavor that I promise it will knock the socks off a 300-pound, steak-loving football player. What's more, you can prepare this after work and have it ready by suppertime. For the best results, don't use extra-lean ground turkey, or the meatloaf will be dry.

---

1 tablespoon olive oil

1 medium red onion, finely chopped

1 red bell pepper, finely chopped

4 garlic cloves, minced

1 tablespoon Neely's Barbecue Seasoning (page 22)

1 teaspoon Old Bay Seasoning

2 tablespoons yellow mustard

2 tablespoons chopped fresh flat-leaf parsley

1 tablespoon Worcestershire sauce

2 teaspoons ground cumin

1 teaspoon salt

½ teaspoon freshly ground black pepper

1 large egg, lightly beaten

1½ cups of Neely's Barbecue Sauce (page 25)

2 cups bread crumbs

2 pounds ground turkey (not extra-lean)

Preheat the oven to 350°F.

Heat the olive oil in a large sauté pan over medium-high heat. Add the onion and bell pepper, and sauté until tender, about 4 minutes. Add the garlic, and cook for another 2 minutes. Remove the skillet from the heat, and allow the mixture to cool completely.

In a large bowl, combine the Neely's Barbecue Seasoning, Old Bay, mustard, parsley, Worcestershire sauce, cumin, salt, pepper, egg, 1 cup of the barbecue sauce, the bread crumbs, and the cooled vegetable mixture. Fold in the ground turkey (do not overmix).

Transfer the meat mixture to a 9 × 13-inch baking dish. Shape the meat into an oblong or rectangular shape (alternatively, you can pat the meat into a buttered 9 × 5-inch loaf pan), gently pressing down on the mixture to eliminate any air pockets. Bake for about 40 minutes. Remove from the oven, and paint the remaining ½ cup Neely's Barbecue Sauce on top of the loaf. Bake in the oven for 20 more minutes.

SERVES 6 TO 8

Thanksgiving Turkey with Lemony Thyme Butter

Gina: These days, with both of us being so busy, Pat usually smokes our holiday hams and turkeys at the restaurant (what can I say, it's a perk of being in the barbecue business), but when we first got married we prepared them at home. Pat and I are holiday people. We love Thanksgiving and Christmas and all the festive traditions associated with each day. It's a special time of year for our families, and Lord knows we have a lot to be thankful for. When it comes to the holiday table, I want the flavor and presentation of everything to be the best. With this bird you can't go wrong. We've been serving it on the Neely holiday table for decades. We hope you enjoy this recipe as much as we do. The flavor, the juicy texture, and, most important, the *love* that inspires it are simply unbelievable.

LEMONY THYME BUTTER
Zest of 1 large lemon
4 garlic cloves
1 cup butter, at room temperature
2 tablespoons Dijon mustard
Juice of 1 large lemon
1 bunch scallions, finely chopped
2 tablespoons chopped fresh thyme
    leaves
2 tablespoons paprika
2 teaspoons salt
1 teaspoon freshly ground black
    pepper

TURKEY
One 14- to 16-pound turkey, rinsed,
    patted dry inside and out (neck,
    heart, and gizzard reserved for
    stock)
Kosher salt
Freshly ground black pepper
3 lemons, cut into 1/8-inch-thick
    slices
4 fresh flat-leaf parsley sprigs
2 fresh rosemary sprigs
2 tablespoons olive oil

To make the thyme butter, blend the lemon zest and garlic in a mini-processor (or a regular food processor) until finely chopped. Add the butter, mustard, lemon juice, scallions, thyme, paprika, salt, and pepper, and process to blend. The butter can be made 2 days ahead. Bring it to room temperature before using.

To roast the turkey, set the rack at the lowest position in the oven and preheat the oven to 325°F.

Transfer 2 tablespoons of the Lemony Thyme Butter to a small bowl; reserve for gravy. Generously season the main turkey cavity with salt and pepper and, using your fingers, coat the cavity with 2 tablespoons of the butter. Starting at the neck end of the turkey, carefully slide your hand between skin and meat of the breast, thighs, and upper drumsticks to loosen the skin. Spread the Lemony Thyme Butter over the meat of the thighs and drumsticks, below the skin, on both sides. Arrange a few lemon slices under the skin. Spread the remaining butter over the breast meat, below the skin. Fill the main cavity with any remaining lemon slices, the parsley, and the rosemary sprigs. Tie the legs together loosely to hold shape. Tuck the wing tips under.

Place the turkey on a rack set in a large roasting pan. Rub the outside of the turkey all over with the oil; sprinkle with salt and pepper. Pour the stock into the pan. Roast the turkey until a thermometer inserted into thickest part of thigh regis-

2 cups turkey stock, Chicken Stock
   (page 28), or water

GRAVY

2 cups (or more) turkey or chicken
   stock (page 28)
2 garlic cloves, thinly sliced
2 shallots, finely chopped
3 tablespoons all-purpose flour
2 tablespoons Lemony Thyme Butter
2 tablespoons fresh lemon juice
½ cup sour cream (optional)
Kosher salt
Freshly ground black pepper

ters 165 to 170°F, about 3 hours. Tilt the turkey so the juices from the main cavity run into the pan. Transfer the turkey to a platter. Tent it very loosely with foil, and let it rest for at least 30 minutes (the internal temperature will rise 5 to 10°). Reserve the juices in the pan.

To make the gravy, scrape the juices and browned bits from the roasting pan into a large glass measuring cup. Spoon off the fat, reserving 2 tablespoons. If necessary, add enough stock to the juices to measure 1⅔ cups.

Heat the reserved 2 tablespoons fat in a heavy, large saucepan over medium-high heat. Add the garlic and shallots; sauté for 2 minutes. Add the flour; whisk until golden, about 4 minutes. Add the degreased pan juices and 2 cups stock. Bring to a boil, whisking until smooth. Reduce the heat and simmer until the gravy is reduced to the desired consistency, about 4 minutes. Whisk in the 2 tablespoons reserved Lemony Thyme Butter, 2 tablespoons lemon juice, and the sour cream, if desired. Season with salt and pepper.

SERVES 10 TO 12

Old-Fashioned Glazed Ham

Gina: In our house, pigs rule (they even have their own room), and we wouldn't have it any other way. We love pork. Adore it. Worship at the pork altar. There are, however, parts of the pig that we favor over others. And ham is at the top of our list.

The key to great ham is the glaze. You've heard Pat go on and on about pulled pork and coleslaw. Well, we feel the same way about ham and glaze: can't have one without the other. Our glaze is a special combination of Creole mustard, dark-brown sugar, and cane syrup. If you put this ham next to the turkey on the holiday table, that bird just might get ignored!

This glaze couldn't be easier to prepare, and it infuses the pork with an incredible flavor. Reason enough to make this ham is the leftovers it will provide—what could be better than thinly sliced ham and mayo on soft white rolls, with a bag of salty potato chips and bottle of cold root beer on the side? That's what I said—nothin'!

1½ cups apple cider
1¼ cups firmly packed dark-brown
    sugar
½ cup Creole mustard (see
    page 93)
¼ cup cane syrup (see page 243)
One 10-pound bone-in ham
Whole cloves for studding

Simmer the apple cider in a small saucepan over medium heat until reduced by one-half; cool to room temperature. Combine the sugar, mustard, cane syrup, and reduced cider in a bowl, and stir to form a thick paste.

Position the rack in the bottom third of oven and preheat the oven to 325°F. Line a large roasting pan with heavy-duty foil, leaving an overhang on all sides. Trim off the skin and all but ¼ inch of fat from ham. Place the ham fat-side up in the prepared pan. Roast the ham until a thermometer inserted in the thickest part registers 130 to 135°F, about 10 minutes per pound.

Remove the ham from the oven; increase the oven temperature to 425°F. Lightly score the fat on the ham in a diamond pattern, and stud the intersection of cuts with whole cloves. Brush glaze thickly over the top and sides of the ham. Return the ham to the oven, and roast until the glaze is deep brown and bubbling, about 25 minutes. Let the ham stand for at least 20 minutes before slicing.

SERVES 10

NOTE: Choose a bone-in ham with the natural shape of a leg. We usually cook with bone-in cuts of meat, whether we're preparing ham, pork shoulder, or rib roasts. The bone not only delivers flavor, but it also holds in juices that tenderize the meat.

Get Yo' Man Chicken

Gina: *Like many of our favorite recipes, this one comes with a story, and, girl, I'm not about to let you down, because this is a tale of seduction. This is one of the recipes I made for Pat when I was courting him (and, most important, his stomach). The key to this dish is the scent it gives off while simmering on the stovetop. The minute your man walks in the house and gets a whiff, well, it's game over (you may not even make it to the dinner table, hon!). It's not a typical Southern dish—the chicken is essentially poached in tomato sauce and fresh herbs—but the end result is chicken that's as tender as any rib that has been smoked for hours over a hickory pit. I use chicken thighs, because the dark meat is flavorful and moist, but you can also use chicken breasts if you are cooking for a breast man (who said that?!?). The result—well, we're still married, aren't we?*

We're not courting anymore, but I still turn to this recipe when I need to get Pat around to my way of thinking—like when he discovers that Gucci bag I've splurged on! Ladies, handle your business and rule the house. Your man will never look at you the same.

---

8 bone-in chicken thighs (or breasts, woo-hoo!), skins removed
1 teaspoon salt
½ teaspoon black pepper
2 tablespoons olive oil
1 medium onion, chopped
1 celery stalk, chopped
½ cup white wine
1 cup Chicken Stock (page 28)
One 14.5-ounce can crushed tomatoes in thick purée
1 tablespoon honey
1 teaspoon red-wine vinegar
2 tablespoons chopped fresh flat-leaf parsley, plus more for garnish
1 tablespoon chopped fresh thyme leaves
1 tablespoon fresh rosemary leaves
Hot buttered rice, for serving (optional)

Rinse the chicken thighs, pat dry with a paper towel, and season with salt and pepper.

Heat the olive oil in a large skillet over medium-high heat. Brown the chicken, meat-side down first, and turn once, cooking about 4 minutes on each side. Transfer to a plate and reserve.

Pour off all but 1 tablespoon of oil from the pan. Add the onion and celery to the skillet, and sauté until tender, about 4 minutes. Add the stock and wine to the pan, and stir, scraping any brown bits off the bottom of the pan; reduce by half, cooking 7 to 8 minutes. Stir in the tomatoes, honey, vinegar, parsley, thyme, and rosemary, and return to a simmer. Add the chicken thighs, turning to coat, then cover, and cook over medium-low heat until the chicken is very tender and pulls easily from the bone, about 40 minutes. Remove the cover, increase the heat to medium, and cook for another 10 to 15 minutes to reduce the sauce. Serve over hot buttered rice, with sauce ladled on top, and garnish with chopped fresh parsley.

SERVES 4 TO 6

Memphis-Style Strip with Beer and Molasses Sauce

Gina: This is Pat's "feel like a king" dish, and if you are married to a meat-and-potatoes man like I am, this dish will make him feel—you guessed it, girl—like a king. The secret to this sauce is two ingredients: bacon and beer. There isn't a man anywhere in Memphis who would turn up his nose at a steak lacquered with both of those. We like to serve this steak sliced on the diagonal, with plenty of extra sauce on the side. When Pat takes a bite of this and gives me one of his sly winks, honey, I know it's a slam dunk!

Three 16-ounce, ½-inch-thick
    prime-aged New York strip
    steaks
3 tablespoons vegetable oil
Kosher salt
Freshly ground black pepper

MOLASSES SAUCE

2 teaspoons butter
2 strips thick-sliced bacon, cut into
    ½-inch pieces
½ medium onion, finely diced
1 garlic clove, minced
1 cup ketchup
¼ cup molasses
¼ cup apple cider
¼ cup lager-style beer
1 tablespoon honey
1 tablespoon prepared yellow
    mustard
1 tablespoon fresh lemon juice
1½ teaspoons Worcestershire sauce
½ teaspoon cayenne pepper
½ teaspoon paprika

Rub the steaks with the oil and season generously with salt and pepper.

Melt the butter in a medium saucepan over medium heat. Add the bacon, onion, and garlic, and sauté for 3 minutes, or until softened. Add the rest of the ingredients, bring to a boil, then reduce the heat to low, and simmer until the sauce is reduced and thickened, 15 to 20 minutes.

Preheat the grill or a grill pan to medium-high. Grill the steaks for about 3 minutes per side for medium-rare; brush the steaks with sauce during the last 2 minutes of cooking time. Allow the steaks to rest for 10 minutes, then slice on the diagonal, and serve with the remaining sauce on the side.

SERVES 6

Deep-Fried Pork Chops and Quick Vegetable Soup

Pat: This is a third-generation Neely dish. Grandma Rena used to cook it for my dad. Then she taught my momma how to prepare it. Now, you know Grandma Rena was a smart woman, showing Momma how to cook for Dad.

Gina: Ladies, this is a very old Southern tactic. My suggestion, if you want to keep your man happy, is to spend some time in the kitchen with his momma and have her teach you a few things.

Pat: I always listen to Gina. You should, too. My momma cooked this dish for my dad and for the kids. Kept us all happy. Now I'm cooking it for my girls (it's one of their favorites on cold-weather days). And I'm sure someday they will cook it for their children.

VEGETABLE SOUP

3 tablespoons butter
2 leeks, white and light-green parts, thinly sliced
2 celery stalks, chopped
2 carrots, chopped
3 tablespoons all-purpose flour
1 tablespoon tomato paste
4 cups Chicken Stock (page 28)
One 14.5-ounce can diced tomatoes
1 large white potato, cubed
1 cup frozen lima beans
1 cup frozen peas
1 cup frozen corn
5 ounces fresh green beans, cut into bite-sized pieces
2 tablespoons chopped fresh flat-leaf parsley, for garnish

PORK CHOPS

Peanut oil, for deep-frying
3/4 cup all-purpose flour
1 tablespoon salt
1 teaspoon black pepper
Four 1-inch-thick bone-in center-cut pork chops

Melt the butter in a large pot over medium heat. Add the leeks, celery, and carrots, and cook, stirring, until softened, 10 to 12 minutes. Sprinkle the flour over the vegetables, and continue to cook, stirring, until the flour reaches a light-blond color. Add the tomato paste, and cook for another minute. Add the stock, and bring the mixture to a boil, stirring occasionally. Add the diced tomatoes and the potato, reduce the heat to low, and simmer until the potato is cooked through, about 20 minutes. The soup can be made up to 1 day in advance.

While the soup is simmering, heat 2 inches of peanut oil in a large Dutch oven to 325°F. Place the flour in a large casserole dish, and season with salt and pepper. Dredge the chops in the flour mixture, patting off the excess. Place the chops, two at a time, in the hot oil, and fry until cooked through, about 6 minutes. Transfer the cooked chops to a paper-towel-lined baking sheet, and repeat with the remaining chops.

Add the cooked chops to the soup and simmer over medium-low heat for another 30 minutes, or until the meat from the chops falls off the bone. During the last 10 minutes of cooking, add the lima beans, peas, corn, and green beans. To serve, ladle the soup into wide, shallow bowls, and garnish with the parsley.

SERVES 4, WITH LEFTOVER SOUP

Beer-Braised Sausages and Sweet Peppers

Gina: Lord knows I love a hot, sizzling grilled sausage, but sausage served all by its lonesome is kind of like a basic dress without accessories, you know what I'm saying? A classic is *always* improved by a dash of color and a bit of sass. That's why this dish is a nice change of pace—pork sausages are braised with an array of peppers (in assorted colors and heat levels), onions, beer, and mustard. The resulting sausages and piquant braising liquid are especially good served atop steamed rice, grilled Italian bread, or creamy grits made with cheese.

1 tablespoon canola oil

Four 4-ounce links pork sausage

1 large onion, thinly sliced

1 red bell pepper, cut into thin strips

1 yellow or orange bell pepper, cut into thin strips

1 or 2 jalapeño or serrano peppers, cut into thin strips

1 yellow Hungarian wax or red Fresno chile pepper (optional), cut into thin strips

2 garlic cloves, very thinly sliced

2 tablespoons Creole mustard (see page 93)

2 tablespoons honey

4 sprigs fresh rosemary (or 1 teaspoon dried rosemary)

1 teaspoon salt

12 ounces amber beer

¼ cup malt vinegar

3 tablespoons chopped fresh flat-leaf parsley

Gina's Perfect Rice (page 27), for serving (optional)

Heat the oil in a large skillet over medium-high heat. Add the sausage, and sear for 5 minutes, turning as necessary, until evenly browned. Transfer to a plate, and add to the skillet the onion, bell peppers, jalapeño, chile pepper, garlic, mustard, honey, rosemary, and salt, and toss well to combine. Add the beer and vinegar, and cook for 1 minute, until slightly reduced. Reduce the heat to low, return the sausages to the skillet, cover, and simmer until the peppers soften, the sausage is cooked through, and the sauce begins to reduce and thicken, 10 to 15 minutes. Stir in the parsley.

Serve the sausage over hot steamed rice, grilled bread, or cheesy grits, if desired, smothered with plenty of the fragrant sauce.

SERVES 4

Pot Roast with Roasted Vegetables

Pat: There is nothing like the smell of a pot roast cooking in the oven. My mother made a mean pot roast; her secret was using dried Italian seasoning on the meat, and it's a technique I've incorporated into this recipe. The flavors of the dressing really permeate and tenderize the roast. A well-seasoned cast-iron Dutch oven (or an enamel-coated Dutch oven) is our favorite cooking vessel for this roast. Here we call for a boneless chuck roast, because the well-marbled cut keeps plenty moist, but you can also use a 4- to 6-pound bone-in roast (you'll need to cook it for another 45 minutes).

Gina: Ladies, this is also a great dish to make when your schedule is tight. You can sear the meat, then throw it and the remaining ingredients into a slow cooker and head off to work. Make some cornbread when you get home, and it's a wrap.

---

2 tablespoons olive oil
One 3- to 4-pound boneless chuck
    roast, trimmed
Kosher salt
Freshly ground black pepper
12 ounces beer (not dark)
1 cup beef broth
One 2-ounce envelope
    Italian-dressing mix
2 bay leaves
10 to 12 garlic cloves, smashed
2 onions, quartered

Preheat the oven to 300°F.

Heat the oil in a large Dutch oven or heavy pot over high heat. Season the pot roast generously with salt and pepper, then add it to the pot, and sear on all sides until nicely brown. Transfer the roast to a plate, then pour the beer into the Dutch oven, whisk to scrape up any browned bits, and whisk down the foam. Stir in the broth, Italian-dressing mix, bay leaves, garlic, and onions. Put the roast back in the Dutch oven, and bake, covered, for 3 hours, or until tender, turning once. Remove the bay leaves, and serve with Roasted Vegetables (recipe follows).

SERVES 6 TO 8

Roasted Vegetables

1½ pounds red new potatoes, halved
1 pound baby carrots
2 medium onions, quartered
2 tablespoons olive oil
1 teaspoon dried thyme
Kosher salt
Freshly ground black pepper
2 tablespoons chopped fresh flat-leaf parsley
2 teaspoons lemon zest
2 tablespoons fresh lemon juice

Preheat the oven to 300°F.

Place the potatoes, carrots, and onions in a large bowl. Add the olive oil and thyme, and season generously with salt and pepper, then toss until the vegetables are evenly coated. Transfer the vegetables to a baking sheet or a large cast-iron skillet, and roast for 45 minutes, or until they are tender and well browned, using a metal spatula to flip them every 15 minutes or so. Remove the vegetables from the oven, cool for 10 minutes, then add the parsley, lemon zest, and lemon juice, and toss to combine. Taste for seasonings, and add more salt or pepper, as desired.

Memphis-Style Barbecued Pork Ribs

Pat: Our first taste of national recognition came in 1997, when our pork ribs were voted "the best ribs in Memphis" by the local media. After the votes were cast, the *Today* show came calling. Tony and I wound up being featured on a segment with Al Roker. Al's enthusiasm for our cooking made others take notice—it was a big moment.

It's important to note that we did not become rib masters overnight. It took time to learn the appropriate techniques. Tender, slow-cooked spare ribs require a certain amount of skill and experience. We got ours, and now we are going to give you yours.

Gina: All I can say about ribs is: Girl, get yourself a man that can grill and let him light it up!

Four 3-pound slabs pork spare ribs (also called St. Louis–style ribs), untrimmed
Kosher salt
2 cups Neely's Barbecue Seasoning (page 22), plus more, as desired
4 cups Neely's Barbecue Sauce (page 25)

Rinse the rib slabs in cold water, and pat dry with paper towels. Place the slabs on a clean chopping board. Using your fingers, pull off the thick white membrane. Use a small knife to trim off the excess fat and meat. Using a sharp knife, trim off the brisket bone (or rib tip). Season both sides of the slab with salt and Neely's Barbecue Seasoning, and refrigerate for at least 1 hour, or up to a day in advance. (See page 166 for illustrated directions.)

When you're ready to cook the ribs, preheat the grill to 250°F, preferably using a combination of hickory wood and charcoal. Place the slab on the grill away from (not directly over) the flame (using indirect heat). Cook the slab curl-side up for approximately 2½ hours. Flip the slab over to finish the cooking, about 1 more hour, or until you get the full "bend" in the slab (see Tony's Tip).

For dry ribs, pull the ribs off the grill, and sprinkle more Neely's Barbecue Seasoning over the entire slab. Cut between the bones and serve. For wet ribs, pull the ribs off the grill, and pour Neely's Barbecue Sauce over the slab. Slice between the bones into individual portions, and serve.

SERVES 6

Memphis-Style Rib Tips

Pat: One of the first lessons we learned in the restaurant business was to waste nothing.

Gina: Use it or lose it. That's the Neely motto.

Pat: Take the brisket bone, or rib tip, for example. It's normally discarded from the spare rib. At Neely's, however, it has become another distinctive menu item. We call rib tips the "rich man's neck bone," because the gristle and fat make this cut of meat rich and flavorful. We cook ours slowly and gently—it keeps them moist and tender.

Once cooked, rib tips can be chopped into bite-sized pieces and are often served as an appetizer. They can be found on restaurant menus all over the country, but they are particularly popular in Chicago, where they are served atop a basket of fries. These bite-sized chunks of tender meat can also be served as an entrée. I have been known to bring home a pound or two to eat with any leftover vegetable that Gina may have prepared the night before.

Gina: Do you see why I married this man??? The things he can do with a rib tip!

---

2 pounds pork rib tips
Kosher salt
½ cup Neely's Barbecue Seasoning
    (page 22)
2 cups Neely's Barbecue Sauce
    (page 25)

Rinse the rib tips in cold water, then pat dry with paper towels. Season all sides of the tips with salt and Neely's Barbecue Seasoning, and refrigerate for at least 1 hour, preferably for up to 8 hours in the refrigerator. Preheat the grill to 250°F, preferably using hickory and charcoal. Place the tips on the grill, away from the flame, using indirect heat. Cook the tips meat-side down first, for 2 hours, then flip and cook for 1½ more hours. The tips should bend (see Tony's Tip, page 165), and the meat will flake and separate when done. To finish, brush the tips with a generous amount of Neely's Barbecue Sauce 15 minutes before removing from the grill.

SERVES 3 OR 4

TONY'S TIP Rib tips might not be available at all grocery stores. You'll have better luck at meat markets.

Barbecued Chicken

What's the secret to our barbecued chicken? We marinate it in Italian dressing! Then we cook it *low and slow*—that's chicken with the Neely brothers' touch. I love to cook chicken in two halves, because the bones and carcass help keep it moist. You can always cut it into individual pieces once it's done. I can guarantee you a great bird if you use our dressing, but feel free to use bottled Italian dressing in a pinch.

Two 3- to 4-pound chickens, halved lengthwise (or 4 whole bone-in chicken breasts, or 10 bone-in thighs or legs)
1 cup Zesty Italian Dressing (recipe follows)
2 tablespoons Neely's Barbecue Seasoning (page 22)
1 cup Neely's Barbecue Sauce (page 25), plus more for serving

Rinse the chicken halves in cold water, and pat dry with paper towels. Place the chicken in a large bowl or baking dish, coat with the Zesty Italian Dressing, and dust with Neely's Barbecue Seasoning. For best results, allow the chicken to marinate in the fridge for at least 2 hours, or overnight.

Thirty minutes before you're ready to cook the chicken, take it out of the fridge and allow it to come to room temperature, then preheat the grill to 250°F, preferably over hickory and charcoal. Place the chicken halves on the grill, cavity-side up. Cover the grill, and cook for about 50 minutes. Flip the chicken over, and cook until it turns golden brown, and the wing and drumstick become very tender and pull easily away at the joints, another 15 to 20 minutes. Brush the chicken with Neely's Barbecue Sauce during the last 5 minutes of cooking, and serve with additional sauce.

SERVES 6 TO 8

Spice Mix and Zesty Italian Dressing

This lively dressing begins with a wonderful spice mix. Make two batches: one to have on hand for several batches of salad dressing, the other to use as a seasoning for grilled or roasted chicken.

SPICE MIX

1 tablespoon garlic salt

1 tablespoon onion powder

1 tablespoon sugar

2 tablespoons dried oregano

1 teaspoon freshly ground black pepper

1 teaspoon dried thyme

1 teaspoon dried basil

1 tablespoon dried parsley

¼ teaspoon celery salt

2 tablespoons Cajun seasoning

ZESTY ITALIAN DRESSING

¼ cup white-wine vinegar

⅔ cup olive oil

2 tablespoons water

2 tablespoons spice mix

In a small bowl, whisk together the garlic salt, onion powder, sugar, oregano, pepper, thyme, basil, parsley, celery salt, and Cajun seasoning. Store the spice mix in a tightly sealed container, and use as needed. To prepare the dressing, whisk together the vinegar, olive oil, water, and 2 tablespoons of the spice mix.

MAKES ABOUT 1 CUP

Sweet and Tangy Pork Chops

Tony: One of the most important skills for any grill master is knowing when a cut of meat is cooked to the desired temperature. This is particularly important when it comes to pork chops, because they can dry out quickly if they're overcooked. Technology has made this easier, with the advent of instant-read meat thermometers, but Lord knows we've all been in situations where the thermometer has gone missing, and then what happened? Dad burned the chop! Which is why we recommend all cooks acquaint themselves with the Neely "feel test."

Gina: Tony's just like Pat, always feelin' things in the kitchen. I tease all the brothers about this, call them the "Feely Neelys." And this is supposed to be a family cookbook!

Tony: Most of us rely on sight and smell in the kitchen, Gina, but you gotta learn to feel as well, especially when grillin'. One surefire way of testing chops and steaks for doneness is our feel test, and it couldn't be easier to master: All you need is a hand and a finger. Here's what you do: Relax your left hand and turn it palm-side up. Now take the index finger of your right hand and poke at the soft area of flesh below the thumb on the left hand. Note the give in the flesh. That's how a cut of meat with an internal temperature of rare (cool, red center) will feel. Now open up your palm, extending the fingers on your left hand. Again, take the index finger of your right hand and poke at the area of flesh below the thumb on the left hand. The flesh will be somewhat tauter, but it will still have some give. That's how a cut of meat with an internal temperature of medium (warm, pink center) will feel. Now stretch the fingers on your left hand as far as they will go, tightening the hand and fingers as if they were a rubber band stretched to capacity. Again, take the index finger of your right hand and poke at the area of flesh below the thumb. See how tight that is, how little give there is. That's a well-done steak. So there you have it: Rare feels fleshy, medium is taut but still has some give, and well done is tight as a drum. Next time your steak is on the grill, give it a poke.

Gina: You can even poke at your gal, tell her you're practicing (but make sure you say that her backside is tight as a drum)!

Four 1-inch-thick bone-in center-cut
    pork chops
Kosher salt
½ cup Neely's Barbecue Seasoning
    (page 22)
2 cups Neely's Barbecue Sauce
    (page 25)

Season the chops with salt and Neely's Barbecue Seasoning, and refrigerate for at least 1 hour. About 30 minutes before you are ready to cook the chops, take them out of the fridge and allow them to come to room temperature.

Preheat the grill to 250°F, preferably over hickory and charcoal.

Place the chops on the grill away from the flame, using indirect heat, and cook for about 45 minutes, turning once. Wrap the chops in a foil packet, and return them to the grill or place them in a 180°F oven, and cook until they are very tender and pull easily away from the bone, about 40 minutes more. Brush the chops with a generous amount of sauce during the last 10 minutes of cooking, then serve them with additional sauce.

SERVES 4

TONY'S TIP Most of us know how to cook chops on the grill: Season the meat, throw the chops down on the grill grate over direct heat, and flip them once (the hotter the grill, the better). But the above method, cooking with indirect heat, also works well. And if you cook over indirect heat, the best way to finish the meat is in a foil wrap, to keep it as juicy and tender as can be. I don't insist on a standard thickness for chops, because my guests have their own preferences. My daughter Madison loves thin pork chops—she won't even eat a thick one—so that's what I prepare for her. But if Pat is coming over, I grill a nice thick chop for him, because that is what he loves.

Barbecued Shrimp

These sweet, tangy shrimp are served in the shell. You gotta peel them to get to the good stuff, so be sure to serve them with plenty of napkins.

4 wooden skewers, soaked in water for 30 minutes
1 pound extra jumbo shrimp (16 to 20 count), with shells on
Kosher salt
3 tablespoons Neely's Barbecue Seasoning (page 22)
2 cups Neely's Barbecue Sauce (page 25), plus more for serving

Heat the grill to 250°F.

Thread the shrimp onto the soaked skewers, and place them in a shallow dish. Sprinkle both sides of shrimp with salt and Neely's Barbecue Seasoning. Place a sheet of aluminum foil on the grill over direct heat. Place the skewers on the foil, and grill for about 3 minutes on each side, until the shrimp are firm and just cooked through (do not overcook). Brush both sides of the shrimp with Neely's Barbecue Sauce, cook for another minute, and then serve with additional sauce on the side.

SERVES 4

TONY'S TIP Barbecued shrimp, catfish, and most other seafood don't need to be seasoned in advance, because their sweet, delicate flavor easily absorbs *plenty* of kick from the grill and the barbecue seasonings and sauce. That's why I sprinkle fish and seafood with seasoning just before grilling. Be sure to place seafood on a sheet of foil, so the it cooks gently and releases juices that will prevent it from sticking to the foil.

Barbecued Catfish

Pat: The sweet, tangy flavor of barbecued catfish is an itch that needs to be scratched fairly often in the Neely house. Like Tony, I usually prepare too much, but leftovers make great sandwiches the next day (especially on grilled white rolls). Be sure to serve this fish with a generous dollop of homemade tartar sauce, our Sweet and Spicy Slaw (page 90), and warm buttermilk biscuits on the side.

Four 6-ounce catfish (ask for U.S., farm-raised catfish) or tilapia fillets
Vegetable oil, as needed
Kosher salt
4 tablespoons Neely's Barbecue Seasoning (page 22)
1 cups Neely's Barbecue Sauce (page 25)
1 recipe Tartar Sauce (recipe follows)

Brush both sides of the fillets with oil, and sprinkle both sides with salt and Neely's Barbecue Seasoning. Preheat the grill to medium-high. Place a sheet of aluminum foil on the grill (away from the coals), and place the fillets directly on the foil. Grill for about 5 minutes total, turning once. Brush the fish with sauce during the last 2 minutes of cooking. Serve with Tartar Sauce and more Barbecue Sauce on the side.

SERVES 4

Tartar Sauce

1 cup mayonnaise
½ cup Dijon mustard
3 tablespoons chopped fresh flat-leaf parsley
3 tablespoons chopped scallion
3 tablespoons drained capers
3 sweet gherkins (we like Mt. Olive brand)
1 tablespoon gherkin juice
3 tablespoons fresh lemon juice
¼ teaspoon kosher salt
⅛ teaspoon cayenne pepper

Mix all the ingredients together in a small bowl. Cover with plastic wrap, and refrigerate for at least 1 hour before serving.

MAKES ABOUT 1⅓ CUPS

Show-Stealing Sandwiches

Pat: Sandwiches tend to fall into two categories: those that are hastily assembled and eaten on the run, and those given lavish attention and savored like a meal. The former often results in a forgettable experience, but the latter, which is how we Neelys approach sandwiches, creates a mix of tastes and textures as satisfying as a four-star meal—and a lot more fun to eat. When it comes to sandwiches, you need to start with good ingredients: the best-quality meats and cheeses, as well as condiments and spreads that perk up flavor, like pickled peppers, hot-pepper jelly, full-flavored cheeses, fresh herbs, and black olive paste, and great bread (crackly baguettes,

crunchy Italian rolls, soft grilled pitas, or tender buns). We also obsess about condiments. (You've heard the saying "Clothes make the man." In Memphis, "Condiments make the sandwich!!") So it's no surprise that you'll find us stirring together our own sweet-pickle mayo, or making sauces from spicy mustard, or infusing yogurt with fresh mint. When it comes to the finish, we reach for the crispest lettuce, and ripe tomatoes seasoned with salt and pepper.

This chapter includes hearty creations that rely on distinctive ingredients: crisp-fried catfish, grilled lamb, smoky pulled pork, and different kinds of burgers from the ones you might be used to. Even our lighter options, like the Grilled Vegetable Hero and Nutty Turkey Salad (chock-full of nuts, cheese, and fruit), will satisfy voracious appetites.

You'll also find our favorite recipes for sandwiches made from ham and turkey leftovers (you can also make them with store-bought deli meats).

Our advice is: Get serious about what you put between the slices of bread, and make your next sandwich a meal!

Grilled Vegetable Hero with Pickled Peppers and Provolone

This zippy Italian-style hero proves that a vegetable sandwich can be as hearty as one made with meat. We take colorful slices of grilled, lightly charred vegetables, an oil-and-vinegar dressing, tapenade (a pungent black-olive spread), fresh basil, and provolone cheese, and serve the whole things on a crackly seeded roll that will keep its texture while soaking up the delicious dressing. This satisfying sandwich is delicious with spiced Terra sweet-potato chips.

2 zucchini, sliced lengthwise into ¼-inch strips

2 yellow summer squash, sliced lengthwise into ¼-inch strips

2 large red or orange bell peppers, quartered lengthwise, seeded

1 medium red onion, sliced into ¼-inch strips

3 tablespoons red-wine vinegar

½ cup extra-virgin olive oil, plus extra for drizzling

Four 8-inch Italian sandwich rolls (preferably with seeds), split lengthwise

Kosher salt

Freshly ground black pepper

6 tablespoons tapenade (or other black-olive spread)

8 thin slices provolone cheese

¼ cup thinly sliced pickled banana peppers

24 whole basil leaves

Heat the grill or a grill pan to medium-high. Arrange the zucchini, squash, bell peppers, and onion on a rimmed baking sheet. Whisk together the vinegar and olive oil in a medium bowl to blend. Brush the cut side of each roll with a small amount of the dressing mixture, then toss the vegetables with remaining dressing, and season with salt and pepper. Grill the cut side of the rolls until toasted, about 1 minute. Place the rolls cut-side up on plates.

Grill the vegetables until tender and lightly charred, turning and brushing occasionally with any dressing mixture left on the baking sheet, about 10 minutes.

Spread the bottom half of each roll with 1½ tablespoons tapenade, and top with the warm vegetables. Cover the vegetables in each sandwich with two slices of cheese, and a quarter of the banana peppers and basil. Finish with an additional drizzle of olive oil and a pinch of salt and pepper.

Cover each sandwich with the top of roll, and press down gently to meld the flavors.

MAKES 4 SANDWICHES

Fried Catfish Sandwich with Sweet Pickle Mayonnaise

Pat: This is our take on a po' boy, one of the defining sandwiches of the South. We take a hot, crispy cornmeal-crusted catfish fillet and slather it with a piquant (easy to make) sweet-pickle mayo, then toss some tart pickles, seasoned tomatoes, and shredded lettuce onto a hoagie roll. This is a meal that's more than a sandwich—it's a masterpiece!

Vegetable oil, for frying
Six 6-ounce catfish fillets (ask for
    U.S., farm-raised catfish)
2 teaspoons Neely's Barbecue
    Seasoning (page 22)
Kosher salt
Freshly ground black pepper
1 cup milk
1 large egg
1 tablespoon hot sauce, plus more
    for serving
1 cup yellow cornmeal
½ cup all-purpose flour
Pinch cayenne pepper
6 hoagie rolls
1 recipe Sweet Pickle Mayonnaise
    (recipe follows)
2 ripe tomatoes, sliced
Iceberg lettuce, thinly sliced
Lemon wedges, for serving

Heat 1 inch of oil in a large skillet to 375°F.

Preheat the oven to 350°F.

Season both sides of the catfish with Neely's Barbecue Seasoning, salt, and black pepper. In a wide bowl, whisk together the milk, egg, and hot sauce. In a pie dish, stir together the cornmeal, flour, cayenne, and a generous sprinkling of salt and pepper.

Dip the catfish in the milk batter, allowing any excess to drip off each fillet, then dredge the fillets in the cornmeal mixture. Transfer the fillets to a baking sheet, and repeat until all the fillets are coated. When you're ready to fry the fish, gently drop the fillets in the skillet (in batches, to avoid overcrowding). Fry the fish for 3 to 4 minutes, until golden and beginning to curl slightly. Drain the fillets on a paper-towel-lined plate, and sprinkle with a little more salt while they are still hot.

Slice each hoagie in half and toast.

To assemble the sandwiches, spread both sides of each toasted hoagie with Sweet Pickle Mayonnaise. Add the catfish and the tomato slices, and top with lettuce. Serve immediately with hot sauce and lemon on the side.

MAKES 6 SANDWICHES

Sweet Pickle Mayonnaise

3/4 cup mayonnaise

2 tablespoons sweet pickles, diced
small

1 shallot, minced

1 tablespoon Creole mustard
(see page 93)

1 tablespoon drained capers,
coarsely chopped

1 tablespoon chopped fresh parsley

2 teaspoons lemon zest

Pinch salt

Pinch freshly ground black pepper

Stir all the ingredients together in a small bowl, cover with
plastic wrap, and refrigerate until needed.

MAKES 1 SCANT CUP

Nutty Turkey Salad

Gina: Red grapes, chunks of provolone cheese, and crunchy almonds give this smoked-turkey salad more personality than the old-school mayo-based options. For added color and crunch, toss the salad with a few handfuls of field greens, so they get coated in the creamy dressing.

Serve this salad on soft whole-grain sandwich bread or ciabatta rolls.

1¼ pounds smoked-turkey breast, diced
Kosher salt
Freshly ground black pepper
1 cup chopped scallions
¾ cup chopped celery
⅓ cup mayonnaise
2 tablespoons Dijon mustard
1 cup seedless red grapes, cut in half
8 ounces provolone cheese, cut into ½-inch cubes
½ cup sliced almonds, toasted and coarsely chopped
3 tablespoons chopped fresh flat-leaf parsley
2 tablespoons snipped fresh chives

Place the turkey in a medium mixing bowl and season with salt and pepper. Add the scallions, celery, mayonnaise, mustard, grapes, provolone, almonds, parsley, and chives, and fold together with a rubber spatula until well combined. Serve immediately, or cover with plastic and refrigerate until needed.

SERVES 6

Memphis Muffuletta

New Orleans is one of our favorite "kick back" vacation destinations. We go there for the people, the food, the music, and the overall vibe. New Orleans is second only to Memphis in vibeness. We also go there for the sandwiches, and always make a point of digging into one of their most famous, the muffuletta, every time we visit. It's a killer sandwich, made with spicy Italian meats, cheeses, and a knockout marinated olive salad, the aroma of which is so powerful that when you're waiting in line it'll cause you to salivate!

Our Memphis Muffuletta has bayou roots for sure. We start with a large round Italian loaf with a sturdy texture, so it can hold up to the delicious mix of ingredients. The meats and cheeses vary, but our favorite is a muffuletta with salami, hot soppressata, mortadella, smoked turkey, Swiss, and aged provolone. Our Memphis kicker is the addition of smoky piquillo peppers from Spain. They infuse the piquant olive salad with an incredible flavor. When it comes to cheese, we go for two flavorful varieties—an imported Swiss and an aged provolone.

We call this our backyard sandwich, because it's actually best if you assemble it in advance and allow it to marinate for about 30 minutes on the cutting board. Then you can cut the big loaf into eight wedges and have dinner on the patio. In New Orleans tradition, serve this sandwich with a cold Abita beer and some spicy Zapp's potato chips.

¾ cup mayonnaise

¼ cup olive oil

3 tablespoons red-wine vinegar

1 tablespoon honey

1 tablespoon fresh lemon juice

½ teaspoon crushed red-pepper
flakes

½ teaspoon dried oregano

Freshly ground black pepper

1 red onion, diced

1 carrot, diced

1 cup diced black olives

1 cup diced green olives

½ cup diced marinated artichoke
hearts

1 cup diced piquillo peppers

½ cup diced celery

⅓ cup chopped fresh flat-leaf
parsley leaves

Kosher salt

1 muffuletta or round Italian loaf
(10 to 12 inches in diameter)

2 ounces each thinly sliced Genoa
salami, hot soppressata,
mortadella, and smoked turkey

2 ounces each thinly sliced
imported Swiss cheese and aged
provolone

Whisk together the mayonnaise, olive oil, vinegar, honey, lemon juice, red-pepper flakes, oregano, and 1 teaspoon black pepper in a large bowl. Add the onion, carrot, olives, artichoke hearts, peppers, celery, and parsley; toss, and season to taste with salt and black pepper. Cover with plastic, and allow the salad to marinate in the refrigerator for at least 1 hour.

Slice the bread in half, and pull some of the interior from the middle of the roll to make room for the other ingredients. Spread a generous amount of the olive oil salad on each half (you will probably have some salad left; it holds for 2 or 3 days in the refrigerator).

Layer the meat and cheese on the bottom half, alternating layers of each meat with thin layers of cheese. Cover with the top half of bread, press gently, slice into wedges, and serve.

SERVES 8

Pulled Pork Sandwiches with Slaw

Pat: When you think of the *defining* Memphis sandwich, there is only one that comes to mind: barbecued pulled pork. In the South, someone always has a grill going in the backyard with a pork shoulder or a Boston butt resting over the coals. As far back as I can remember, there were big black drums with charcoal smoke rolling out of the stacks. (We've even got bumper stickers down here that say, "Honk if you love it pulled.") So it was no wonder that when Neely's opened, our pulled-pork sandwich became the number one seller. Now we have customers who come several times a week and order a supersized pulled pork sandwich with a supersized side of Neely's baked beans. Of course, you can't serve a pulled-pork sandwich without coleslaw. A mound of hickory-smoked pulled pork slathered with our barbecue sauce and topped with coleslaw, on a toasted bun—well, this is arguably not only a Memphis signature, it's one of the world's best sandwiches.

For spectacular results, marinate the pork in the dry rub one day in advance; this allows the seasonings to permeate the meat, producing an outstanding flavor.

One 10- to 12-pound pork shoulder
  or Boston butt
3 tablespoons Neely's Barbecue
  Seasoning (page 22)
3 tablespoons coarsely ground black
  pepper
2 tablespoons kosher salt
12 soft hamburger buns, split
Neely's Barbecue Sauce (page 25)
3 cups Sweet and Spicy Slaw, about
  ½ recipe (page 90)

Mix together the Neely's Barbecue Seasoning, pepper, and salt. Rinse the shoulder or butt thoroughly, pat dry with paper towels, and massage the seasoning mixture into the meat. Cover the meat with plastic wrap, and refrigerate for at least 2 hours or up to 1 day in advance.

Following the manufacturer's instructions, and using lump charcoal and ½ cup of soaked wood chips for the smoker (or 1 cup for a kettle grill), start a fire, and bring the temperature of the smoker or barbecue grill to 275°F.

Place the pork on a rack in the smoker or on the grill. Cover, and cook the meat until a thermometer inserted into the center registers 165°F, turning the pork every hour or so, about 6 hours total. Add more charcoal as needed to maintain the temperature, and more drained wood chips to maintain the smoke level.

Transfer the pork to a rimmed baking sheet (this is important—you'll want to catch all the flavorful juices), and allow it to stand until cool enough to handle. Shred the pork into bite-sized pieces, and mound on a platter. Pour any juices from the baking sheet over the pork. At this point, the pork can be served immediately, or covered with foil and refrigerated for a day. If you chill the pork, rewarm it, covered, in a in 350°F oven for about 30 minutes.

To assemble the sandwiches, mound the pork on the buns, paint a little Neely's Barbecue Sauce on the pork, top with coleslaw, and cover with bun top. Insert into mouth, taste. See what I mean? *The best sandwich ever!*

SERVES 12

TONY'S TIP If you don't have time to watch coals for 6 hours, you can also place the pork on the grill for an hour or so, then transfer the meat to a slow-cooker or a low oven for another 3 to 4 hours, until it is falling-apart tender. Or you can forget the grill and simply cook the shoulder in the slow cooker for 5 to 6 hours. It won't have the smoke, but it will have the tenderness.

Memphis Monte Cristo

Pat: The Monte Cristo is a coffee-shop staple, a sandwich made with ham, turkey, and Swiss cheese, dipped in batter, and fried until golden. It appears in different guises across the country, and, depending on where you order one, it can also be served grilled, deep-fried, or open-faced. We've given this sandwich a Neely spin, layering ham, smoked turkey, and Muenster cheese on white sandwich bread and adding hot-pepper jelly as a finish. We fry ours, then dust it with confectioners' sugar, creating a delicious play of salty and sweet flavors and crispy and gooey textures. A spoonful of fresh peach preserves is a delicious condiment for this sandwich.

8 slices white sandwich bread
½ cup hot-pepper jelly
8 slices cured ham
8 slices smoked turkey
8 slices Muenster cheese
2 large eggs
Splash half-and-half
Dash hot sauce
Pinch salt
2 tablespoons butter
Confectioners' sugar, for garnish
Peach preserves, for garnish
 (optional)

Place four slices of bread on the counter and spread 2 tablespoons of pepper jelly on each. Add ham, turkey, and cheese to each sandwich, and top with the remaining slices of bread. Beat the eggs with the half-and-half, hot sauce, and salt in a medium bowl. Heat a griddle pan or a skillet over medium heat. Melt 1 tablespoon of the butter in the skillet. Dip two sandwiches in the egg batter, allowing any excess to drip off, and fry for 3 to 4 minutes on each side, until golden brown and crisp. Repeat with the remaining two sandwiches.

To serve, slice the sandwiches in half diagonally, dust with confectioners' sugar, and serve with a spoonful of peach preserves.

SERVES 4

Lamb Souvlaki with Creamy Yogurt Sauce

Souvlaki (Greek-style kebabs) is our kind of food. Marinated meat and vegetables are grilled on a skewer. The skewers can be assembled in minutes, and the flavors are light, fresh, and satisfying. You can make souvlaki with any kind of meat, but we love the flavor of marinated lamb best. Grilled peppers and onions prove to be wonderful partners here, especially when they are served in warm pita bread with a generous dollop of mint-flavored yogurt sauce.

LAMB

¼ cup olive oil
1 pound boneless lamb leg, cut in 2-inch dice
2 teaspoons kosher salt
2 teaspoons chopped fresh rosemary leaves
1 teaspoon Neely's Barbecue Seasoning (page 22)
½ teaspoon freshly ground black pepper
½ teaspoon ground cumin
¼ teaspoon crushed red-pepper flakes

YOGURT SAUCE

1½ cups plain whole-milk yogurt
1 medium cucumber, peeled, seeded, and finely chopped
½ teaspoon minced garlic
2 tablespoons chopped fresh mint leaves
2 tablespoons olive oil
Kosher salt

SKEWERS

4 wooden skewers, soaked in water
1 large red bell pepper, cut in 2-inch dice
Kosher salt
1 medium red onion, cut into large (2-inch) dice
4 large (8-inch) rounds pita bread
1 ripe tomato, diced
Lemon wedges, for serving

Combine the olive oil, lamb, salt, rosemary, Neely's Barbecue Seasoning, black pepper, cumin, and red-pepper flakes in a medium bowl. Use your fingers to toss the meat with the seasonings until it is evenly coated. Refrigerate the meat for at least 15 minutes, or preferably overnight.

While the meat is marinating, make the yogurt sauce. Stir together the yogurt, cucumber, garlic, mint, olive oil, and a pinch of salt in a medium bowl. Cover with plastic wrap, and refrigerate until needed.

When you're ready to cook the lamb, heat the grill to medium-high or turn on the broiler. Place the lamb, bell pepper, and onion on the four soaked skewers, and sprinkle lightly with salt. Grill over hot coals, or cook under the broiler, turning as necessary to cook evenly, about 5 minutes for medium-rare.

When the lamb is cooked, throw the pita rounds on the grill to warm and soften. To serve, place one skewer in each piece of bread, fold the pita like a baseball glove, and remove the skewer from the meat. Top each sandwich with yogurt sauce and diced tomato, and serve with wedges of lemon.

MAKES 4 SANDWICHES

Memphis Blues Burgers with Mustard Sauce

Pat: You can shape these burgers into four ¼-pound patties, but in Memphis, we shape them into mini-burgers so each person gets to eat two (and kids love the easy-to-eat size). Drizzled with a spicy mustard sauce and topped with ripe tomatoes, pickles, and fresh lettuce, these juicy, satisfying burgers fly off the plate every time. Run out of these and you'll be singing the Memphis blues.

1 small red onion, cut into ¼-inch slices
1 pound ground beef
½ small onion, grated
¼ teaspoon salt
¼ teaspoon freshly ground black pepper
8 small potato rolls, split in half
2 medium-sized ripe tomatoes, sliced
Sliced pickles, for garnish
Leaf lettuce, for garnish
1 recipe Mustard Sauce (recipe follows)

Preheat a flat-top grill pan to high.

Place the sliced onion on the grill, and cook until lightly charred and tender, about 10 minutes.

In a medium bowl, combine the ground beef, grated onion, salt, and pepper. Make eight small burgers equal in size, about 3 inches across.

Cook the burgers on the flat-top for 3 to 4 minutes on each side. Serve on the split rolls with grilled onions, tomatoes, pickles, and Mustard Sauce.

SERVES 4

NOTE: To really "blues" up your burgers, top them with crumbled blue cheese.

Mustard Sauce

3 tablespoons mayonnaise
1 tablespoon Dijon mustard
1 teaspoon apple-cider vinegar
¼ teaspoon cayenne pepper
Kosher salt
Freshly ground black pepper

Stir all the ingredients together in a small mixing bowl.

MAKES ¼ CUP

Turkey Burgers with Grilled Tomatoes and Lemon Mayonnaise

Pat: You know I like my burgers, but who ever thought that a burger could taste this good and be so healthy? My turkey-burger recipe (a favorite with the ladies) is a mixture of ground turkey, fresh marjoram, crushed red-pepper flakes, and garlic. The key to making these burgers taste as good as the old reliable is to use ground turkey that is 85 percent lean. This will yield an incredibly satisfying (and still virtuous) patty. Grilled tomatoes, silky avocado, and a sunny lemon condiment help keep the burger moist.

TURKEY BURGERS

1½ pounds ground turkey
    (85 percent lean)
2 tablespoons chopped fresh
    marjoram or oregano
1 tablespoon chopped fresh flat-leaf
    parsley leaves
2 scallions, finely chopped
1 garlic clove, minced
1 teaspoon kosher salt
½ teaspoon crushed red-pepper
    flakes
½ teaspoon freshly ground black
    pepper

Vegetable oil, for brushing patties
1 large tomato, cut into ¼-inch
    slices
½ cup Lemon Mayonnaise (recipe
    follows)
4 English muffins, split in half and
    toasted
Leaf lettuce, for garnish
1 ripe avocado, thinly sliced, for
    garnish

Use your hands to mix the ground turkey, marjoram, parsley, scallions, garlic, salt, red-pepper flakes, and black pepper in a medium bowl; do not overmix or the burgers will be tough. Shape the meat into four patties, each about ¾-inch thick, and set them on a plate. Cover with plastic, and refrigerate for at least 30 minutes or for up to 8 hours.

Thirty minutes before you're ready to grill the turkey patties, remove them from the refrigerator. Heat the grill to medium-high. Lightly brush the patties with oil, and grill over direct heat for 4 to 5 minutes on each side, until just cooked through. (Do not overcook burgers or they will dry out.) Brush the grill with additional oil, then grill the tomato slices until they are lightly charred, 1 to 2 minutes per side, and use a metal spatula to remove them from grill.

Serve the burgers on the toasted muffins with the grilled tomatoes, Lemon Mayonnaise, lettuce, and sliced avocado.

SERVES 4

Lemon Mayonnaise

½ cup mayonnaise

2 teaspoons Creole mustard
  (see page 93)

1 teaspoon grated lemon zest

1 teaspoon fresh lemon juice

Combine the ingredients in a small bowl, cover with plastic, and refrigerate until needed.

MAKES ½ CUP

Day-After Turkey and Ham Sandwiches

Pat: Let's face it, one of the great joys of roasting a big ole turkey or ham is the leftovers. Can you imagine what the day after Thanksgiving would be like without a big turkey sandwich? Anytime we have leftover ham, I dream of ham sandwiches on a soft roll with a little dollop of Miracle Whip. When it comes right down to it, I think I prefer the sandwiches to the actual meal.

What follows are two of our favorite ways to dress up leftovers. The Turkey, Brie, and Cranberry Panini are crisp and cheesy and have become a year-round lunch staple. The warm ham-and-egg biscuits are satisfying any time of day.

Turkey, Brie, and Cranberry Panini

1 tablespoon olive oil
2 tablespoons softened butter, plus more for focaccia
1 large onion, thinly sliced
1 teaspoon fresh thyme leaves (optional)
Kosher salt
Freshly ground black pepper
8 slices rosemary focaccia or other dense, soft-crumbed Italian bread
12 to 16 ounces thinly sliced roast turkey (or smoked turkey)
8 thick slices Brie (about 6 ounces)
½ cup whole cranberry sauce (see note)

Heat the olive oil and butter in a medium skillet over medium-high heat. When the fat starts to sizzle, add the onion, thyme, and a pinch of salt and pepper, reduce the heat to medium-low, and cook, stirring, until the onion slices are caramelized and golden, 12 to 14 minutes. Remove from the heat, and cool slightly.

Heat a panini press to medium-high. To assemble the sandwich, butter one side of a focaccia slice and place it butter-side down on grill. Top with 3 or 4 ounces of turkey, a spoonful of onion, 2 slices Brie, and a slather of cranberry sauce. Top with the remaining slice of focaccia, butter the top, and place the sandwich on the grill. Carefully lower the grill over the top, to press the sandwich together neatly, and grill until golden, 3 to 4 minutes. Repeat to make the other sandwiches.

SERVES 4

NOTE: For the neatest results, drain the cranberry sauce before spreading on the sandwiches.

Scrambled Egg, Bacon, and Ham Biscuits with Pepper Jelly

Gina: This recipe calls for four Momma Daisy's Buttermilk Biscuits, but a batch makes ten, so you're going to have a few left over. This is never a bad thing. You can have them for breakfast the next day, and the next, and then when you run out you can make another batch!

8 strips thick-sliced bacon
8 large eggs
2 tablespoons half-and-half
½ teaspoon kosher salt
Several grinds black pepper
Dash or two hot sauce
2 tablespoons butter
¾ cup chopped ham (about
    4½ ounces)
2 tablespoons snipped fresh chives
¼ cup hot-pepper jelly
4 warm Momma Daisy's Buttermilk
    Biscuits (page 236), split in half

Cook the bacon over medium heat in a large cast-iron skillet until crisp, and transfer to a plate lined with paper towels. Drain all but 1 tablespoon of bacon fat from the skillet.

Whisk together the eggs, half-and half, salt, pepper, and hot sauce in a medium bowl.

Return the skillet to medium-low heat. Add the butter to the skillet, and heat until it begins to bubble, then stir in the eggs. Use a rubber spatula to push the eggs toward the center of the skillet, tilting the skillet to allow the liquid to run underneath the dry portions. When the eggs are almost set, stir in the ham and chives, and remove from the heat (the eggs will continue to cook).

To assemble the sandwiches, spread 1 tablespoon of pepper jelly over the bottom half of each biscuit. Divide the eggs evenly among the four biscuits, then top with two strips of bacon and the remaining biscuit halves, and serve.

SERVES 4

The Sweet Life: Our Favorite Desserts

Pat: Southerners love their sugar. I suppose that's why I'm so at home here in Memphis. As far back as I can remember, my family never went *anywhere* that there wasn't a cake plate to greet us. Anytime you visited anyone, there would be something sweet in the house, and this wasn't just in our home, it was in *every home* in the South.

At my grandma Rena's, for instance, there would always be a frosted layer cake, an apple pie, or a big, buttery pound cake waiting for us. She'd serve the cake or pie with homemade ice cream (made from the old wooden churn that you cranked by hand). So we loved going to Grandma Rena's.

My grandmother on my mother's side, Momma Daisy, was also a baker, famous for her banana pudding and cobbler. We loved visiting her as well. And back in those days, most folks had peach and pecan trees in their yard, so desserts made from those ingredients were very popular, and still are. You simply cannot deny Southerners their desserts.

This sweet tradition was passed down to my mother, who made us cakes, cookies, even a molded Jell-O dessert with whipped cream that was absolutely delicious—and we never had a meal without ice cream (a tradition that haunts me as an adult). My mother's aim was not to spoil us, but to make sure we were sated and happy. With six kids and limited resources, she was always worried about cooking enough food.

These days, the sweet traditions carry on. We cook, and we cook dessert, though we don't always eat it after supper. Mornings might find me having a warmed piece of Sock-It-to-Me Cake with my coffee. And in the middle of the night, I've been known to sneak downstairs for a scoop of ice cream—served atop a warm brownie or drizzled with warm butterscotch sauce. Shelbi and Spenser suffer the same affliction: They are dessert-crazy, and go hog-wild for buttermilk cupcakes and coconut cake.

The recipes in this chapter are homey, delicious, and unapologetically Southern. A few of our desserts are best made in advance so they can *chill* (Momma Daisy's Banana Pudding, Frozen Lemonade Pie), which make them great options when you're entertaining. Finally, we have a few dazzlers for special occasions, such as the striking three-tiered Southern Red Velvet Cake or Mississippi Mud Cake. After tasting a few of these, you'll understand why folks in the South say, "You come to dinner for the desserts!" 🐖

Key Lime Bars

Gina: These tart-sweet bar cookies are a variation on traditional lemon bars, and, girl, they are a vacation in a pan! The tender cookie base holds a puckery lime filling that gets a little extra kick from grated lime zest. You can use fresh limes or that bottled Key-lime juice you brought back from your last trip to the Gulf Coast. These bars need nothing more than a dusting of confectioners' sugar, and they make an ideal dessert for barbecues, picnics, and slumber parties.

COOKIE CRUST
1 cup unsalted butter
½ cup confectioners' sugar
2 cups all-purpose flour
Pinch kosher salt

LIME TOPPING
4 large eggs, lightly beaten
2 cups sugar
6 tablespoons all-purpose flour
¼ cup plus 2 tablespoons fresh lime juice (or bottled Key-lime juice)
2 teaspoons grated lime zest
Confectioners' sugar, for garnish

Preheat the oven to 350°F.

Spray the bottom and sides of a 9 × 13-inch cake pan with nonstick spray.

To make the crust, combine the butter and confectioners' sugar in the bowl of an electric mixer fitted with the paddle attachment. Beat on medium-high speed for 2 to 3 minutes, until light and fluffy. Add the flour and salt, and mix another minute, until well combined (see note). Transfer the dough to the prepared pan, and pat out to an even thickness over the bottom of the pan. Bake the crust for 20 to 25 minutes, until lightly golden. Remove from the oven, and cool on a baking rack.

To make the topping, whisk together the eggs and sugar in a large mixing bowl. Add the flour, and whisk until just combined, then whisk in the lime juice and zest. Pour the lime topping over the cooled crust, then bake for an additional 25 minutes, or until the filling is set.

Allow the bars to cool completely. Generously dust with confectioners' sugar and cut into squares. For the neatest presentation, use a metal spatula or a butcher's scraper to remove the bars from the pan. Leftovers will keep for 2 or 3 days at room temperature, or for up to a week in the refrigerator.

MAKES 16 TO 20 BARS

NOTE: The cookie crust dough can be prepared up to 2 days in advance, then wrapped in plastic and stored in the refrigerator. When you're ready to bake the bars, simply bring the dough to room temperature and pat out as described above.

Candy Bar Brownie Crunch

Pat: We all have our vices, and mine is brownies—particularly these brownies, which have candy bars and crunchy pecans baked right in. They are some of the most decadent brownies you will ever eat. When I have one of these at two in the morning, I'm tempted to let out a loud moan, but then Gina would probably throw me out.

Gina used to make them for me when we were courting—hence the seductive additions. They say that chocolate is an aphrodisiac, so if you're looking for a sweet deal to spark a little romance in your house, take my advice: Light a fire, add the Whipped Cream, fresh raspberries, and silky chocolate shavings, and you'll be well on your way to a blissful ending!

1 cup unsalted butter, plus more for greasing
4 ounces unsweetened chocolate
1 cup all-purpose flour
½ teaspoon baking powder
¼ teaspoon salt
2 cups sugar
4 large eggs
1 teaspoon pure vanilla extract
1 cup coarsely chopped pecans
10 chocolate-caramel-covered wafers (we use Twix bars), chilled
1 recipe Chocolate Ganache (recipe follows)
1 recipe Whipped Cream (recipe follows)
Fresh raspberries
Chocolate shavings

Preheat the oven to 325°F. Butter and flour an 8 × 8-inch baking pan.

Melt the butter and chocolate over low heat in a medium, heavy saucepan, stirring occasionally. When the chocolate has melted, remove from the heat and cool for 10 minutes.

Meanwhile, sift together the flour, baking powder, and salt into a mixing bowl and set aside.

In a medium bowl, use a wooden spoon to beat the sugar and eggs together until well combined, about 2 minutes. Slowly pour the sugar-egg mixture into the cooled chocolate, stirring constantly, then stir in the vanilla. Add the flour mixture and stir just until the dry ingredients disappear (do not overmix).

Place the pecans and the chilled candy bars in a food processor, and pulse until coarse chunks form. Spread half of the brownie batter into the pan, top evenly with the pecan-and-candy-bar mixture, then cover with remaining batter. Bake for 35 to 40 minutes, or until a toothpick inserted in the center of the brownies comes out clean. (While the brownies are baking, make the Whipped Cream, so it has time to chill.) Remove the brownies from the oven, and cool completely. Run a paring knife around the rim of the brownies to loosen from pan.

Drizzle the brownies with ganache, and set them aside for 30 minutes, until the ganache sets. Then cut the brownies into squares, and garnish with Whipped Cream, fresh raspberries, and chocolate shavings.

SERVES 8 TO 10

NOTE: If time is of the essence, you can also make this recipe using a 21-ounce box of brownie mix. Prepare the brownies as directed on the box for "cakelike" brownies, using three eggs total. The brownies will cut neater if you allow the ganache to set for at least 30 minutes once it is spread on the brownies. Be sure to chill the candy bars before chopping them, so they don't turn to mush in the food processor.

Chocolate Ganache

½ cup heavy cream
2 tablespoons light corn syrup
4 ounces best-quality bittersweet chocolate, finely chopped

Warm the cream in the microwave, or in a small saucepan over medium heat, until it is very hot but not boiling. Combine the corn syrup and chocolate in a mixing bowl. Pour the hot cream over the chocolate mixture, and let it sit for 2 minutes to allow the chocolate to melt. Stir until the chocolate is completely melted, and the mixture is smooth.

Whipped Cream

2 cups heavy cream
½ cup confectioners' sugar
1 teaspoon vanilla extract

Beat the cream in a bowl with an electric mixer at medium speed until it becomes frothy. Add the sugar and vanilla; continue beating until the cream holds soft peaks. Do not overbeat. Refrigerate the cream, covered with plastic wrap, for no more than 1 hour if not using immediately.

Shelbi's Pig Butter Cookies

Gina: When it comes to hanging with our girls, no place beats our kitchen. Shelbi and Spenser love to cook, have always enjoyed spending time in the kitchen, from an early age. Shelbi in particular loves to bake, and these delicate butter cookies are one of her (and our) favorites. As I often mention on our show, I am a big collector of all things piggy, and if you come for a visit in my kitchen you'll see HOW BIG! You can cut these cookies into any shape you choose, but in our house we choose to cut them into the shape of a—oink, oink—pig (pig cutter shapes can be found online or at specialty baking stores).

3¾ cups all-purpose flour, plus more for work surface
¾ teaspoon salt
1¾ cups unsalted butter, softened
1¼ cups confectioners' sugar
2 teaspoons pure vanilla extract
Coarse pink decorating sugar (optional)

Sift together the flour and salt onto a sheet of parchment paper on your work surface.

Place the butter in the bowl of an electric mixer fitted with the paddle attachment, and beat on medium-high speed until fluffy and light, about 2 minutes. Add the sugar and vanilla, and mix until combined. Reduce the speed to low, and slowly add the flour and salt to the butter-and-sugar mixture, mixing until the batter is smooth. Turn the dough out onto a sheet of plastic wrap. Cut the dough into quarters, and wrap each quarter in plastic, then chill in the refrigerator for 2 hours.

When you're ready to bake the cookies, preheat the oven to 350°F. Line two 9 × 13-inch baking sheets with parchment paper.

Using a rolling pin dusted with flour, roll out one of the dough quarters (keeping the others refrigerated until you need them), on a lightly floured work surface, to a ¼- to ⅛-inch thickness. Cut the cookies into the desired shapes, then use a metal spatula to transfer the cookies to one of the prepared baking sheets (the cookies should be about 1½ inches apart). Sprinkle the cookies with decorating sugar, if desired.

Repeat with remaining dough, and bake the cookies until they are lightly golden, about 8 minutes. Cool briefly in the pan, then use a metal spatula to transfer the cookies to a wire rack to cool completely.

MAKES ABOUT 2 DOZEN PIGS

NOTE: Shelbi tells me that the cookies will cut out neater if you dip the cutters in flour, then tap them gently to knock off any excess.

Momma Daisy's Peach and Blackberry Cobbler

Pat: When it comes to summertime in the South, fresh peaches rule. We put them in ice cream, pie, and cobbler. We pack them in mason jars and cover them with syrup. No getting around it: we have never met a peach-and-sugar dish that we didn't like.

When we were kids, Momma Daisy had several peach trees in her backyard. She'd give my brothers and me a big basket, and we would go out and pick them right off the tree. Next thing you knew, she was making cobbler—man, was that a treat. Needless to say, that was always a fun trip, and now we get to relive it by sharing her recipe with you.

BISCUIT TOPPING

2 cups all-purpose flour, plus more
    for work surface
¼ cup cornmeal
¼ cup plus 2 tablespoons
    granulated sugar
1 tablespoon baking powder
½ teaspoon salt
2 tablespoons cold unsalted butter,
    plus more for baking dish
2 tablespoons vegetable shortening
1 cup whole milk
1 large egg, lightly beaten

PEACH FILLING

2 pounds fresh peaches, peeled,
    pitted, and sliced (or 2 pounds
    frozen sliced peaches, thawed)
1 cup firmly packed light-brown
    sugar
2 teaspoons fresh lemon juice
2 tablespoons cornstarch
½ teaspoon ground cinnamon
Pinch salt
1 teaspoon pure vanilla extract
2 pints fresh blackberries (or
    10 ounces frozen blackberries,
    unthawed)
Vanilla ice cream, for serving

To make the biscuit topping, in a large bowl, whisk together the flour, cornmeal, ¼ cup sugar, baking powder, and salt. Cut in the butter and shortening until the mixture resembles coarse crumbs. Using a fork, stir in the milk and egg just to combine (do not overmix). Set aside while preparing the filling.

To make the peach filling, preheat the oven to 350°F. Generously butter a 7 × 11-inch baking dish.

Heat the peaches, brown sugar, lemon juice, cornstarch, cinnamon, and pinch of salt in a medium saucepan over medium-high heat. Bring the peaches to a boil, stirring frequently. Reduce the heat to medium-low and simmer, stirring, until the sauce thickens and the peaches have softened, about 5 minutes. Remove from the heat, and stir in the vanilla and blackberries. Transfer the filling to the prepared baking dish.

Use a spoon to scoop approximately 2 tablespoons of batter and use another spoon to place the batter on top of the fruit mixture. Continue with the remaining batter, covering the fruit evenly. Sprinkle the tops of the biscuits with the remaining 2 tablespoons granulated sugar, and bake for 25 to 30 minutes, or until the biscuits are golden brown and the filling is bubbly and thick around the edges.

Cool for 10 minutes, then serve warm with ice cream.

SERVES 6 TO 8

NOTE: If you use frozen blackberries, do not thaw them, and toss them with 2 tablespoons of flour before combining them with the peaches.

Frozen Lemonade Pie

Pat: This cool, creamy pie is as refreshing as a glass of lemonade—and it goes down just as easy. We use lemonade concentrate, sweetened condensed milk, and whipped cream to create a fluffy, light-textured filling, then cradle the filling in a graham-cracker crust and freeze the pie before serving. The result is a beat-the-heat, not-too-heavy dessert that can easily follow a big feast—and still disappear (not that anyone in our family is ever too full for dessert!).

The lemon-zest garnish is not essential, but it sure is beautiful and fun to make, and it adds another little kiss of lemony love.

GRAHAM-CRACKER CRUST

2 cups graham-cracker crumbs (see note)

¹⁄₄ cup sugar

7 tablespoons unsalted butter, melted

LEMONADE FILLING

One 14-ounce can sweetened condensed milk, chilled

One 12-ounce container Cool Whip topping

One 6-ounce can frozen lemonade concentrate, thawed

1 tablespoon finely grated lemon zest

1 recipe Candied Lemon Zest, for garnish (recipe follows)

Preheat the oven to 350°F.

In a medium bowl, stir together the graham-cracker crumbs, sugar, and melted butter, until the mixture resembles wet sand. Transfer the crumb mixture to a 10-inch glass pie plate, and pat out to an even thickness. Bake the crust for 7 minutes, until fragrant and lightly golden, and then cool completely on a wire rack.

Using a rubber spatula, gently fold the chilled sweetened condensed milk and Cool Whip together in a medium bowl. Gently fold in the lemonade concentrate (do not overmix or the mixture will become soupy). Pour the mixture into the graham-cracker crust, mounding it as high as possible, and freeze overnight. Serve straight from the freezer, garnished with Candied Lemon Zest and cut into wedges.

MAKES ONE 9-INCH PIE

NOTES: You might have a spoonful or two of extra lemonade filling. If that's the case, by all means, freeze it in a small cup or baking dish for a lemonade "mousse" snack for the cook.

We use prepared graham cracker crumbs for this crust, because it's so easy to buy them already ground. If you prefer to use the crackers, you'll need to blend about eight of them to make 2 cups total. Using a food processor, just pulse the crackers until the mixture is in coarse crumbs, add the sugar and melted butter and pulse until finely ground, then transfer the mixture to the pie pan.

Candied Lemon Zest

2 lemons, well scrubbed
1 cup sugar, plus more for rolling
½ cup cool water

Use a vegetable peeler to remove the zest from the lemons, keeping the strips as long as possible. Use a paring knife to remove the bitter white pith from the zest, and discard. Using a sharp chef's knife, finely julienne the strips of zest, and then place them in a small bowl. Cover the zest with boiling water; let stand for 30 minutes, then drain.

Heat the sugar and cool water in a small saucepan over medium-high heat. Bring the mixture to a boil, stir until the sugar is completely dissolved, then add the julienned zest. Reduce the heat to medium-low, and cook for 10 minutes. Remove from the heat, cover, and let stand at room temperature overnight. Remove the zest, and drain on wire rack. Roll the zest in the sugar. Dry on a wire rack. The zest can be stored in an airtight container for up to 2 weeks.

Strawberry Rhubarb Pie with Crumbly Oat Topping

Gina: One is juicy and sweet, the other sassy and tart, and the glue that holds them together? Plenty of sugar! Strawberry and rhubarb are made for each other, kinda like Pat and me. I love this pie because there is just one crust to roll, the filling is a snap, and the crumbly topping adds another layer of sweet crunch as it bakes down into the fragrant fruit filling. The result is a pie that's as much fun to eat as a bar cookie.

SWEET PIE DOUGH

1½ cups plus 2 tablespoons all-purpose flour, plus more for work surface

2 tablespoons sugar

½ teaspoon salt

8 tablespoons cold unsalted butter, cut into small pieces

2 tablespoons vegetable shortening

3 to 4 tablespoons ice water, or as needed

FILLING

¾ pound rhubarb, sliced ½ inch thick on sharp diagonal (3½ to 4 cups)

Two 1-pint baskets strawberries, hulled, halved

1 cup sugar

2 teaspoons grated orange zest

¼ cup fresh orange juice

¼ cup cornstarch

½ teaspoon ground cinnamon

⅛ teaspoon freshly grated nutmeg

OAT TOPPING

⅔ cup plus 2 tablespoons rolled oats

½ cup all-purpose flour

½ cup pecans

½ cup firmly packed light-brown sugar

To make the crust, pulse the flour with the sugar and salt in a food processor. Add the butter and shortening, and pulse just until the mixture resembles coarse meal. Add the ice water, and process until a dough just starts to form. Transfer the dough to a floured work surface, and knead gently. Pat the dough into a disk, wrap in plastic, and refrigerate for at least 1 hour. (The crust can be prepared 1 day ahead. Soften slightly at room temperature before rolling out.)

On a lightly floured work surface, roll out the dough to an 11-inch round about ¼ inch thick. Transfer the dough to a 10-inch ceramic or glass tart pan, and roll a rolling pin over the pan to trim the overhang. Using a fork, prick the bottom of the pie shell all over, and refrigerate until firm, at least 20 minutes.

Preheat the oven to 350°F.

Line the shell with foil, and fill with pie weights or dried beans. Bake for about 20 minutes, or until lightly golden around the edge. Remove from the oven, and gently remove the foil and the weights.

To make the filling, combine the rhubarb, strawberries, sugar, orange zest, orange juice, cornstarch, cinnamon, and nutmeg in medium saucepan. Set aside while you prepare the oat topping.

Increase the oven temperature to 375°F.

To make the topping, combine ⅔ cup of the oats, the flour, pecans, brown sugar, and cinnamon in a food processor fitted with a metal blade. Pulse to mix. Add the butter, and pulse until the mixture becomes crumbly. Transfer the mixture to a medium bowl. Stir in the remaining 2 tablespoons oats.

Heat the rhubarb mixture over medium heat. Bring the

½ teaspoon ground cinnamon

6 tablespoons chilled unsalted butter, cut into ½-inch pieces

Vanilla ice cream, for serving (optional)

mixture to a boil, stirring constantly, then reduce the heat to low, and simmer until the rhubarb is tender and the mixture has thickened, about 8 minutes; set aside to cool.

After the filling has cooled, transfer it to the baked shell. Sprinkle with the oat topping, pressing it gently into the fruit mixture. Bake for an additional 20 to 25 minutes, until the topping is golden brown and the filling is bubbling to the surface. Serve the pie warm or at room temperature, with vanilla ice cream.

SERVES 8

FIRST ROW: Spenser in a high school photo; The Glamour Girls:
Spenser, Gina, and Shelbi; Shelbi
SECOND ROW: Shelbi and Spenser on summer vacation in Destin,
Florida; Dad feeding Shelbi her favorite birthday cake
THIRD ROW: Spenser feeding little sister Shelbi; Spenser and
Shelbi on a cruise vacation

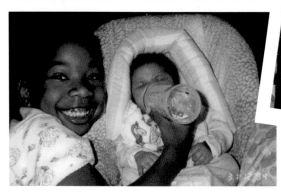

Calley's Sweet Potato Pie

Gina: Calley Anderson is Shelbi's best friend, in large part because Belinda Anderson, Calley's mother, is my best friend. Calley is an excellent student but the girl is a chef at heart. Baking is her first love, and one day Calley made this sweet potato pie for our family, and it knocked me off my feet. The filling relies on two sweeteners, brown sugar and maple sugar, for an incredible flavor. Warm spices and pure vanilla create an intoxicating perfume, and fresh lemon juice helps cut the sweetness and balance the flavors. So, I swallowed my pride (along with another slice of pie) and asked her for the recipe. Here I am, an adult asking my daughter's friend for a recipe—pretty funny, huh?

---

1 recipe Sweet Pie Dough
    (page 210)

FILLING

4 medium-large sweet potatoes
    (about 3 pounds)
½ cup heavy cream
½ cup firmly packed light-brown
    sugar
¼ cup maple syrup
3 large eggs, lightly beaten
2 tablespoons unsalted butter,
    melted
2 teaspoons pure vanilla extract
2 tablespoons fresh lemon juice
½ teaspoon kosher salt
½ teaspoon ground cinnamon
¼ teaspoon ground allspice
¼ teaspoon grated nutmeg
⅛ teaspoon ground ginger

Vanilla ice cream or whipped
    cream, for serving

Prepare the dough as directed on page 210.

Preheat the oven to 375°F.

On a lightly floured work surface, roll out the dough to an 11-inch round about ¼ inch thick. Transfer the dough to a 9-inch pie dish, and trim the overhang to ¾ inch; fold the overhang under itself and crimp decoratively. Using a fork, prick the bottom of the pie shell all over, and refrigerate until firm.

Remove the pie shell from the fridge, line with foil, and fill with pie weights or dried beans. Bake the shell for about 20 minutes, or until lightly golden around the edges. Remove the foil and the weights, and bake for about 12 minutes longer, or until the pie shell is golden brown and cooked on the bottom (cover the rim of the pie shell with foil if it starts to get too brown). Remove the pie shell from the oven and cool completely on a baking rack. Leave the oven on.

Prick the sweet potatoes with a paring knife, and bake them for 1 hour, or until tender; cool slightly. Slit the skins, and scoop the potato flesh into a bowl. Use a whisk to mash until smooth. Whisk in the cream, brown sugar, maple syrup, eggs, butter, vanilla, lemon juice, salt, cinnamon, allspice, nutmeg, and ginger, and scrape the filling into the pie shell.

Bake the pie for 15 minutes. Turn the oven down to 350°F, and continue to bake for about 40 minutes longer, or until the filling is set. Transfer the pie to a wire rack to cool. Serve warm or at room temperature with vanilla ice cream or whipped cream.

MAKES ONE 9-INCH PIE

Sock-It-to-Me Cake

Gina: This is Momma Neely's calling card (and when Momma Neely comes calling, people answer). It's a traditional Southern butter cake filled with pecans and cinnamon and finished with a light sugar glaze. At the restaurant, this dessert rules the house!

You can serve it with ice cream at the end of a meal, or for breakfast with coffee to start your day. When Patrick gets to the restaurant early in the morning, it's the first thing he reaches for. Our recipe yields an extremely moist and delicious yellow cake. It will knock your socks off!

Nonstick cooking spray

STREUSEL FILLING
2 tablespoons brown sugar
2 teaspoons ground cinnamon
1 cup coarsely chopped pecans

YELLOW CAKE
2¼ cups cake flour
1½ cups sugar
1 tablespoon baking powder
1 teaspoon salt
½ cup vegetable oil
1 cup milk
1 teaspoon vanilla extract
1 teaspoon fresh lemon juice
2 large eggs unbeaten

GLAZE
¼ cup confectioners' sugar
2 tablespoons milk
2 tablespoons fresh lemon juice

Preheat the oven to 350°F.

Coat a 9 × 13-inch baking pan with nonstick cooking spray.

To make the streusel filling, combine the brown sugar, cinnamon, and pecans in a small bowl, and set aside.

To make the cake, sift the cake flour, sugar, baking powder, and salt together in the bowl of an electric mixer. Add the oil, ¾ cup of the milk, the vanilla, and lemon juice, and, using the paddle attachment, beat for 2 minutes at high speed.

Add the remaining ¼ cup milk and the eggs; beat for 2 minutes longer. Pour two-thirds of the batter into the prepared pan. Sprinkle the batter evenly with the streusel filling, then spoon the remaining batter evenly over the filling. Bake for 28 to 33 minutes, or until a toothpick inserted in the center of the cake comes out clean. The cake will bounce back when lightly touched with a finger. Allow the cake to cool for 25 minutes in the pan. Run a knife around the edges, invert onto serving plate or cooling rack, and cool completely.

To make the glaze, whisk together the confectioners' sugar, milk, and lemon juice in a small bowl until smooth. Drizzle the glaze over the cooled cake.

MAKES ONE 9 X 13-INCH CAKE

Sour Cream Pound Cake with Warm Raspberry Syrup

Gina: Calling all ladies to the kitchen! This is my absolute fa-vo-rite!!! It's a sour-cream pound cake, but, girl, here's the surprise: After you bake it, you need to *grill* it. (That barbecue man got me crazy, huh?)

Resist the temptation to use a box mix for this one, because a cake made from scratch will give you the best flavor. I'm all for mixes now and then, especially with everybody's busy schedule, but, you know, sometimes we have to *slow it down* and enjoy the fruits (and warm fruit toppings) of our labor. So fire up that grill pan, slice that cake, and brush it with *butter* (no margarine!) on both sides. The cake, toasted, will take on those great grill marks and be ready to stand up to a scoop of vanilla ice cream, a generous drizzle of Warm Raspberry Syrup, and any other sundae-style toppings that grab you (pass the crumbled Oreos and M&M's!). When you finally place that plate in front of your man, you can have anything you want afterward—*anything*!

You can also dress this dessert in a fancy outfit by cubing the cake and layering it with ice cream and Warm Raspberry Syrup in a parfait glass.

CAKE

1½ cups unsalted butter, at room temperature

3 cups sugar

6 large eggs, at room temperature

1 teaspoon vanilla extract

1 teaspoon lemon extract

1 teaspoon almond extract

2 teaspoons grated lemon zest

2 teaspoons grated orange zest

3 cups all-purpose flour

½ teaspoon kosher salt

¼ teaspoon baking soda

1 cup sour cream

Vanilla ice cream, for garnish

Warm Raspberry Syrup (recipe follows), for garnish

Preheat the oven to 350°F. Grease and flour a 3-quart Bundt pan.

In the bowl of an electric mixer fitted with the paddle attachment, cream 1 cup of the butter and the sugar together at medium-high speed until light and fluffy, 2 to 3 minutes. Add the eggs, one at a time, beating well after each addition. Add the vanilla, lemon and almond extracts, and grated zests, and mix well. In a medium bowl, sift together the flour, salt, and baking soda. Add a third of the dry mixture to the creamed mixture, and beat on low until mixed. Mix in half of the sour cream. Alternate adding the flour mixture and the sour cream. Pour the cake batter into the prepared Bundt pan. Bake for 60 to 70 minutes, or until a cake tester inserted in the center of the cake comes out clean. Cool for 15 minutes, then invert the cake onto a wire rack, remove from the pan, and cool completely.

Heat a grill pan to medium-high. Melt the remaining ½ cup of butter, and slice the cake into wedges at least 1½ inches thick. Using a pastry brush, brush both sides of each slice with butter. Grill the slices on both sides until golden brown, about 3 minutes total. Remove from the grill pan. Cool slightly, and

Toppings such as chocolate M&M's, crumbled Oreos, toasted nuts, chopped fresh kiwi fruit or pineapple, chocolate syrup, and/or whipped cream (optional)

serve topped with vanilla ice cream and Warm Raspberry Syrup.

To create sundaes, cut cake slices into bite-sized pieces. Layer parfait glasses with ice cream and cubes of cake, sprinkle on desired toppings, and drizzle with Warm Raspberry Syrup.

SERVES 6 TO 8

Warm Raspberry Syrup

Because the berries are simmered whole and not strained, this sauce has a chunky texture.

3 cups raspberries

1 tablespoon fresh lemon juice

6 tablespoons sugar

2 tablespoons raspberry or
    red-currant jelly

1 tablespoon cognac or other brandy

Heat all the ingredients in a small saucepan over medium heat, and let simmer for 5 minutes. Let cool slightly, and then serve warm.

MAKES ABOUT 3 CUPS

Strawberry Shortcut Cake

Gina: Oh boy. When I realized the importance of Strawberry Shortcut Cake to the Neely boys, I knew I had to get baking and learn this recipe! The first step was getting permission from Momma Neely to make the cake. Let's just say baking the cake was the easy part!

Momma Neely always brought this cake to our house on special occasions. Didn't matter if the occasion was a birthday, a graduation, or a good report card. It got to the point where our girls would say, "I need to call Grandma Neely and tell her about my report card so she can bring me some shortcut cake." I like to call it a shortcut cake because we use a boxed mix. But no one will ever be able to tell when you serve it.

Butter, for greasing
¼ cup all-purpose flour, plus more
    for greasing
One 18.25-ounce box strawberry
    cake mix
3 large eggs
1 cup water
⅓ cup vegetable oil
3 cups fresh strawberries, sliced,
    plus more for garnish
2 tablespoons cognac
¼ cup granulated sugar
1 cup heavy cream
¼ cup confectioners' sugar
1 teaspoon vanilla extract
One 3-ounce package
    strawberry-flavored Jell-O

Preheat the oven to 350°F. Butter and flour a 13 × 9 × 2-inch non-stick cake pan.

In the bowl of an electric mixer fitted with the paddle attachment, beat together the cake mix, flour, eggs, 1 cup water, and the oil at low speed until mixed well. Increase the speed to medium-high, and beat for another 4 minutes, until the batter is smooth and glossy.

Pour the batter into the pan, and bake for 35 to 40 minutes. Cool the cake on a wire rack.

While the cake cools, combine the strawberries, cognac, and granulated sugar in a medium bowl, and allow them to set for 20 minutes. Pour the cream into a bowl, then add the confectioners' sugar and vanilla, and beat on medium-high until stiff peaks form. Cover the whipped cream, and refrigerate.

Run a butter knife around the rim of the cake. Prepare the Jell-O according to the package instructions, and allow it to chill for at least 20 minutes, until it is thickened but not firm. Using a straw, poke holes all over the cake. Pour the Jell-O on top of the cake and into the holes. Spread the macerated strawberries on top of the cake in an even layer. Use a rubber spatula to spread a layer of whipped cream on top of the strawberries. Garnish with fresh strawberries, as desired, and refrigerate for at least 4 hours. Serve this cake straight from the pan, and refrigerate any leftovers.

SERVES 10 TO 12

Behave Yourself Cupcakes with Chocolate Cream Cheese Icing

Pat: Cupcakes bring out the kid in everyone. They certainly bring out the kid in me, and my girls will tell you that I love these cupcakes as much as they do. Who can blame me? They are impossible to resist. The combination of cake flour and buttermilk gives them a tender crumb and a slightly tangy flavor, and the thick, rich cream-cheese frosting—made with melted chocolate chips—puts them over the top. These cupcakes starred in the "If Pat's a Good Boy" episode of our show. Talk about inspiration to behave!

Gina often doubles this recipe so we have enough around to feed a crowd for a party or picnic, because even when folks are on their best behavior these have a way of vanishing. . . .

Twelve 2½-inch paper muffin-cup
  liners

2 cups cake flour
1 teaspoon baking powder
½ teaspoon baking soda
½ teaspoon salt
2 large eggs, at room temperature
1⅓ cups sugar
½ cup unsalted butter, melted
1½ teaspoons pure vanilla extract
1⅓ cups well-shaken buttermilk
Chocolate Cream Cheese Icing
  (recipe follows)

Preheat the oven to 350°F. Line a 12-cup muffin tin with paper liners.

Sift the flour, baking powder, baking soda, and salt together in a medium bowl. In a large bowl, beat the eggs and sugar together until fluffy. Add the melted butter, vanilla, and the buttermilk. Mix until just incorporated. Pour the sifted dry ingredients slowly into the batter. Mix until just combined and smooth. The batter will appear light and fluffy.

Divide the batter evenly among the muffin cups, and bake for about 18 minutes, or until a toothpick inserted in the center of a muffin comes out clean. Let the cupcakes cool on a wire rack for 10 to 15 minutes before frosting.

MAKES 12 CUPCAKES

Chocolate Cream Cheese Icing

½ cup unsalted butter, softened
One 8-ounce block cream cheese,
  softened
4 ounces semisweet chocolate,
  melted (see note)
3 cups confectioners' sugar, sifted
1 teaspoon vanilla extract
1 tablespoon milk

Beat the butter and cream cheese until creamy. Add the melted chocolate, confectioners' sugar, vanilla, and milk, and beat until the icing is smooth and creamy.

MAKES ENOUGH ICING FOR 12 CUPCAKES

NOTE: Melt the chocolate in a double boiler or in a metal bowl placed over a saucepan of gently simmering water (the bowl should not touch the water).

Coconut Pineapple Bundt Cake

Gina: Multilayered coconut cakes are the prom queens of Southern desserts—and we love them—but, like prom queens, those cakes take time to prepare. This buttery Bundt cake, make with coconut milk, coconut flakes, and fresh chopped pineapple swirled right into the batter, is easier to make and just as satisfying. A pineapple glaze adds a tart punch to the mix.

COCONUT CAKE

1 cup unsalted butter, at room temperature, plus more for greasing

3 cups all-purpose flour, plus more for dusting

3 cups (packed) sweetened flaked coconut (about 10½ ounces)

1 cup chopped fresh pineapple

1 cup walnuts, coarsely chopped

1½ teaspoons baking powder

1 teaspoon baking soda

¾ teaspoon salt

2 cups sugar

6 large eggs

2 teaspoons pure vanilla extract

2 tablespoons crème de cacao

1 cup plus 2 tablespoons unsweetened coconut milk (not low-fat)

PINEAPPLE GLAZE

1¾ cups confectioners' sugar

2 to 3 tablespoons pineapple juice

Preheat the oven to 350°F. Generously butter a 3-quart Bundt pan; dust the pan with flour, shaking out any excess.

In a medium mixing bowl, combine ½ cup of the flour with 2 cups of the flaked coconut, the pineapple, and walnuts; set aside.

Whisk together the remaining 2½ cups flour, the baking powder, baking soda, and salt in a medium bowl. Combine the butter and sugar in the bowl of a standing electric mixer fitted with the paddle attachment and beat until light and fluffy. Beat in the eggs, one at a time, then the vanilla and crème de cacao. Alternately stir in batches of the flour and 1 cup of the coconut milk, beginning and ending with the dry mixture. Fold in the coconut-pineapple-nut mixture. Transfer the batter to the prepared pan and use a rubber spatula to smooth the top.

Bake until the top is golden brown and a tester inserted near the center of the cake comes out clean, about 1 hour and 10 minutes. Cool the cake in the pan for 5 minutes. Turn the cake out onto a wire rack; cool completely.

While the cake cools, place the remaining cup of flaked coconut on a baking sheet, and toast in the oven for 5 to 6 minutes, until golden brown.

To make the glaze, whisk the confectioners' sugar, pineapple juice, and remaining 2 tablespoons coconut milk in a medium bowl to blend. Spoon the glaze over the cooled cake, then garnish with toasted flaked coconut. Allow the glaze to set for at least 15 minutes before serving.

SERVES 10 TO 12

Mississippi Mud Cake

Gina: Just about every church cookbook and family recipe box throughout the South has its own version of this dark, rich chocolate cake named for the "muddy" Mississippi River. In our version, we add coffee to deepen the chocolate flavor, and throw in a handful of mini–chocolate chips, creating a sinfully "muddy" bottom that's fun to drag your fork through. Then we top the whole thing off with mini-marshmallows and a river of icing. This is one Mississippi cake you'll be happy to drown in!

CAKE

1 cup unsalted butter, plus more for greasing
2 cups all-purpose flour, plus more for dusting
2 cups sugar
1 teaspoon baking soda
½ teaspoon salt
½ cup cocoa
½ cup strong brewed coffee
2 large eggs
½ cup buttermilk
2 teaspoons vanilla extract
1 cup mini semisweet morsels
8 ounces miniature marshmallows

ICING

½ cup unsalted butter, softened
3 tablespoons cocoa
2 teaspoons instant espresso crystals
2 tablespoons hot water
½ cup heavy cream
1 pound confectioners' sugar
1 teaspoon pure vanilla extract
1 cup pecans, coarsely chopped, for garnish

To make the cake, preheat the oven to 350°F. Grease and flour a 9 × 13-inch baking pan.

Whisk together the flour, sugar, baking soda, and salt in a large mixing bowl.

Heat the butter, cocoa, and coffee in a medium saucepan over medium-high heat, stirring constantly, just until the butter is melted; remove from the heat, and cool slightly. Stir the dry ingredients into the chocolate mixture until smooth.

In a medium mixing bowl, whisk together the eggs, buttermilk, and vanilla, and then add this mixture to the chocolate batter, stirring until combined. Pour the batter into the prepared pan, and bake for 25 minutes, or until it is springy to the touch and a cake tester inserted in the center of the cake comes out mostly clean. Allow the cake to cool for 5 minutes on a wire rack, then top with the mini morsels and miniature marshmallows.

While the cake is baking, make the icing. Melt the butter with the cocoa, instant espresso, hot water, and cream over medium-low heat. Bring the mixture to a boil, then remove from the heat. Stir in the confectioners' sugar, then the vanilla.

Pour the warm icing over the cake and the chocolate chips and marshmallows, top with the chopped nuts, and cool completely before serving.

SERVES 10 TO 12

Southern Red Velvet Cake

Gina: Red Velvet Cake is beloved throughout the South. It's sweet and moist, with a deep-crimson hue that comes from the addition of red food coloring to the cake batter. In the old days, folks used beets or red cabbage to dye their cakes! Red Velvet is a buttermilk cake, which is one of the reasons it's so moist; there's also cocoa in the batter, which is one of the reasons it's popular with children (that, and the traditional cream-cheese frosting). It's red and white, but it tastes black and white, and it's always a stunner when you cut into one. Making someone a layer cake is an investment. It takes time, hon. But it's also a beautiful, loving gesture, and nicer than any present you can buy. This sexy cake is easier than you might think to assemble, and the results are sure to steal the show at any party.

Nonstick vegetable cooking spray, for pans
2 tablespoons unsweetened cocoa powder, plus more for dusting
5 cups cake flour (not self-rising)
2 teaspoons kosher salt
3 cups sugar
3 cups canola oil
4 large eggs
4 tablespoons red food coloring (one 2-ounce bottle)
2 teaspoons pure vanilla extract
2 cups well-shaken buttermilk
1 tablespoon baking soda
5 teaspoons distilled white vinegar
1 recipe Cream Cheese Frosting (recipe follows)

Preheat the oven to 350°F. Generously spray three 9 × 2-inch round cake pans with nonstick cooking spray, and line with parchment paper. Spray the lining; dust with cocoa, tapping out any excess. Set aside. Whisk together the flour, salt, and cocoa in a medium bowl; set aside.

Mix the sugar and oil at medium speed in the bowl of an electric mixer fitted with the paddle attachment until combined. Add the eggs, one at a time; mix well after each addition. Mix in the food coloring and vanilla. Add the flour mixture in three batches, alternating with the buttermilk, mixing well after each addition. Scrape down the sides of bowl as needed.

Stir together the baking soda and vinegar in a small non-reactive bowl. Add the baking-soda mixture to the batter, and mix at medium speed for 10 seconds. Divide the batter equally among the pans. Tap the pans on the counter to remove bubbles. Bake until a cake tester inserted in the middle of the cake comes out clean, 35 to 40 minutes. Cool the pans on a rack for 5 minutes. Invert the cakes onto wire racks to cool completely.

To assemble, place one layer top-side down on a cake stand. Using an offset spatula, spread with a ¼-inch-thick layer of frosting. Repeat with the remaining layers. To frost the top and sides of the cake, work from the center toward and over the edge, making sure to coat evenly. The cake can be stored in the refrigerator for up to 1 week.

MAKES ONE 3-LAYER 9-INCH CAKE

Cream Cheese Frosting

Three 8-ounce packages cream
 cheese, softened
5 cups sifted confectioners' sugar
1½ cups unsalted butter, softened
1½ teaspoons vanilla extract

In a standing electric mixer fitted with the paddle attachment, or with a handheld electric mixer in a large bowl, mix the cream cheese and butter at low speed until incorporated. Add the sugar and vanilla. Increase the speed to high, and mix until light and fluffy, about 5 minutes, scraping down the sides of the bowl with a rubber spatula as needed.

Store in the refrigerator before using, until it is somewhat stiff, about 15 minutes. The frosting may be stored in the refrigerator for 3 days.

MAKES ENOUGH TO FROST A 3-LAYER 9-INCH CAKE

Late-Night Butterscotch Sundaes with Virginia Peanuts

Pat: The name of this decadent sundae speaks for itself. The recipe serves four, and makes a nostalgic dessert that will drive your dinner guests wild. But I'll tell you something—when that silky sauce is sittin' in the fridge, calling out my name, it serves one! I've already confessed my fondness for late-night desserts, and I can only think of one other thing I'd rather be doing in the middle of the night.

Although you can use any roasted peanuts in this recipe, try to seek out Virginia nuts. They have a crispy snap all their own, and a peanut flavor that can't be beat.

---

1 cup Butterscotch Sauce (recipe
    follows)
¾ cup salted Virginia peanuts,
    coarsely chopped
2 tablespoons Jack Daniel's
1 pint vanilla or chocolate ice cream
Chopped toffee candy bar (such as
    Heath Bar), for garnish

Warm the Butterscotch Sauce in a small saucepan over medium-low heat. Stir ½ cup of the peanuts and the whiskey into the sauce. Scoop ice cream into four sundae dishes, and spoon sauce over the top. Sprinkle the sundaes with the reserved peanuts and with toffee candy.

SERVES 4

Butterscotch Sauce

1 cup firmly packed light-brown
    sugar
½ cup light corn syrup
6 tablespoons unsalted butter
½ cup heavy cream
1½ teaspoons pure vanilla extract
½ teaspoon fresh lemon juice
Pinch salt

Heat the brown sugar, corn syrup, and butter in a small saucepan, and cook over medium-low heat, stirring, until the sugar is dissolved. Bring the mixture to a boil, stirring constantly. Stir in the cream, and remove from heat. Add the vanilla, lemon juice, and salt, and stir to combine. Serve the sauce warm or at room temperature over ice cream. Store leftovers, covered, in the refrigerator for 1 week. Add a few tablespoons of cream or water to loosen, if necessary, when reheating.

MAKES ABOUT 1½ CUPS

Gina and Mom share a special moment in the Pig Room.
This is the girls' hangout.... Not many are allowed access. Oink!

Boozy Baked Apples

Gina: Nothing is as warm or as inviting as an old-fashioned baked apple. Our baked apples are even more inviting because we pack them with golden raisins, dried cranberries, and nuts, splashed with rum for extra goodness (or try Calvados, an apple-flavored liqueur from France, for a special twist).

Serve these warm, fragrant little gems with a scoop of caramel or rum-raisin ice cream. In the unlikely event that you have a few left over, there's nothing like a cold baked apple for breakfast, served in a pool of cold half-and-half. (Chances are your sweet-tooth husband is also on to this secret, so don't be surprised if he beats you to the kitchen.)

Nonstick cooking spray
1/4 cup rum or Calvados
1/3 cup golden raisins
1/3 cup dried cranberries
6 same-sized Granny Smith apples
3/4 cup firmly packed light-brown sugar
3/4 cup coarsely chopped walnuts
4 tablespoons cold unsalted butter, cut into 1/2-inch pieces
1 teaspoon ground cinnamon
1 teaspoon grated lemon zest
1/4 teaspoon grated nutmeg
1/2 cup apple cider or juice
2 tablespoons fresh lemon juice
1 quart vanilla ice cream

Preheat the oven to 375°F. Lightly coat a shallow 8 × 12-inch (or similar-sized) baking dish with nonstick cooking spray.

Gently heat the Calvados, raisins, and dried cranberries in a small saucepan until warmed through; swirl the pan to coat the dried fruit, and set aside to macerate.

Core the apples all the way through with an apple corer, making a 1-inch-wide hole. Peel the upper third of each apple. Using a sharp paring knife, score the flesh about 1/4 inch deep around the circumference, where the peeled and unpeeled areas meet (see note). With the paring knife angled down, cut a shallow crater around the top of the hole to help hold the preserves that will go there. Set aside while you make the filling.

In a medium bowl, combine the brown sugar, walnuts, 2 tablespoons of the butter, the cinnamon, lemon zest, nutmeg, and dried-fruit mixture. Lightly pack the cavities with the fruit mixture. Sprinkle any remaining filling around the apples, pour the apple cider and lemon juice around the apples, and dot with the remaining 2 tablespoons butter.

Bake the apples for 15 minutes, then baste with their juices. Continue to bake, basting regularly, until tender, about 1 hour. Remove from the oven and let stand for about 10 minutes before serving. Transfer the apples to serving bowls, spoon the juices over the top, and serve with ice cream.

SERVES 6

NOTE: Scoring the apples along the circumference minimizes splitting when they are baking.

Sinners' Brunch Peach Crumb Cake

Gina: With a spicy, nutty crumb topping and sweet peaches baked right in, this irresistible crumb cake is a favorite for sleep-late brunches (a good option when you have houseguests and everyone had a little bit too much fun the night before). The cake is easy enough to stir together the morning of the brunch, or the night before. To continue the decadence, consider serving peach Bellinis (peach purée with champagne), along with plenty of eggs, bacon, hash browns, etc.

CAKE

½ cup unsalted butter, at room temperature, plus more for greasing

1¼ cups all-purpose flour, plus more for pan

¾ cup granulated sugar

2 large eggs, at room temperature

½ cup whole milk

1 teaspoon pure vanilla extract

1 teaspoon baking powder

¼ teaspoon baking soda

½ teaspoon kosher salt

3 large peaches (about 1¼ pounds), peeled and sliced thin

CRUMB TOPPING

¾ cup firmly packed light-brown sugar

1 cup pecans, chopped

½ teaspoon ground cinnamon

¼ teaspoon grated nutmeg

¼ teaspoon kosher salt

½ cup unsalted butter, melted

1 cup plus 2 teaspoons all-purpose flour

GLAZE

½ cup confectioners' sugar

2 tablespoons unsalted butter, melted

2 teaspoons whole milk

½ teaspoon pure vanilla extract

Preheat the oven to 350°F. Butter and flour a 9 × 9-inch baking pan.

Cream the butter and sugar in the bowl of an electric mixer fitted with the paddle attachment at high speed for 2 to 3 minutes, until light and fluffy. Reduce the speed to low, and add the eggs, one at a time, then the milk and vanilla. In a separate bowl, sift together the flour, baking powder, baking soda, and salt. With the mixer at low speed, add the flour mixture to the batter until just combined. Fold in the peaches, and stir with a spatula to be sure the batter is completely mixed.

Combine the brown sugar, pecans, cinnamon, nutmeg, and salt in a bowl. Stir in the melted butter and then the flour. Mix well, and set aside.

Spoon the batter into the prepared pan, and spread it out with a knife. Using your fingers, crumble the topping evenly over the batter. Bake for 40 to 50 minutes, until a cake tester inserted in the center of the cake comes out clean.

In a small bowl, whisk together the confectioners' sugar, butter, milk, and vanilla. Using a fork, drizzle the glaze over the warm cake, and cool slightly. Serve warm or at room temperature.

SERVES 8

Yeast Doughnuts with Maple Icing

Gina: Light, delicate, and full of flavor, homemade doughnuts are a true indulgence, one that's worthy of a holiday, a birthday breakfast, or any other special occasion ("Look mom, all A's!"). This recipe takes a bit of advance work, to prepare the dough and allow it to rise, but it's a fun project to do with your kids. And the maple icing makes it difficult to eat just one.

1 tablespoon active dry yeast

½ cup warm water (approximately 115°F)

⅓ cup plus ½ teaspoon sugar

1 large egg, lightly beaten

½ teaspoon salt

½ cup scalded milk

6 tablespoons butter, melted and cooled

About 3½ cups all-purpose flour, plus more for work surface

Vegetable shortening or vegetable oil, for deep-frying

1 recipe Maple Icing (recipe follows)

Combine the yeast, warm water, and ½ teaspoon of the sugar in a small bowl. Set aside until the mixture becomes foamy, about 20 minutes. In the bowl of a standing electric mixer, beat the egg with the remaining ⅓ cup sugar and the salt until the mixture is thick and light.

Beat in the yeast mixture, the scalded milk, and the butter, and gradually add enough flour to form a soft dough. Knead the dough on a floured surface for 1 minute, just until it is smooth and elastic, and form it into a ball. Put the dough in a buttered bowl, cover with plastic wrap, and let it rise in a warm place for 1 hour and 30 minutes, or until it has doubled in bulk.

When the dough has risen, punch it down, and on a floured surface roll it out ⅓ inch thick. With a 2½-inch cutter dipped in flour, cut out rounds. With a 1-inch round cutter dipped in flour, cut out and reserve the centers from the rounds. Gather the scraps gently into a ball, reroll the dough, and cut out doughnuts and holes in the same manner. With a spatula, transfer the doughnuts and holes to a baking sheet sprinkled lightly with flour, and let rise, uncovered, in a warm place for 30 minutes to 1 hour, or until they have doubled in height.

In a large deep fryer, heat 3 inches vegetable shortening or vegetable oil to 360°F. Fry the doughnuts, four at a time, for 1 minute on each side, or until they are golden brown and puffed, then transfer them with a skimmer to paper towels to drain. Fry the doughnut holes separately, turning them to brown evenly.

Dip the doughnuts and holes, one at a time, in the icing, turning them to coat them, and transfer them with tongs to a rack set over waxed paper to dry.

MAKES ABOUT 2 DOZEN DOUGHNUTS

NOTE: Never fry more than four doughnuts at a time, and keep the fat as near to 360°F as possible, without letting it creep too high or fall too low. If the oil is too cool, the doughnuts will absorb too much fat; if it's too hot, the doughnuts will brown before they cook inside.

Maple Icing

3 cups confectioners' sugar
4 to 5 tablespoons milk
¼ teaspoon maple extract
  (available in most grocery stores
  and specialty baking shops)

In a small bowl, combine the confectioners' sugar and 4 tablespoons of the milk; stir well. Add additional milk to reach the desired consistency. Stir in the maple extract.

MAKES 1½ CUPS ICING

Nana's Caramel Pecan Rolls

Gina: I don't know if any of you have an appetizer before breakfast, but that's what we sometimes do in our house, and it sure is fun. 'Course, when we do, the only appetizer we make is Nana's Caramel Pecan Rolls.

Nana was my godmother, who lived across the street from us while we were growing up. Nana is one of the best cooks in our family, and one of our most cherished matriarchs. She took care of me from the time I was six months old until I started school. Later, Nana took care of Shelbi when she was a baby.

Nana always made the best caramel pecan rolls, and when we didn't want to make them ourselves, we'd call her and request a batch for a special Sunday breakfast. After making these, you'll know why.

DOUGH
Two ¼-ounce packages active
    dry yeast
½ cup sugar
¾ cup warm water
2 large eggs
1¼ teaspoons salt
4½ cups flour, plus more for work
    surface
½ cup unsalted butter, melted
Vegetable oil, for greasing

FILLING
1 cup unsalted butter, softened
¾ cup firmly packed light-brown
    sugar
1 tablespoon ground cinnamon
1 cup pecans, chopped
½ cup raisins

Combine the yeast, 1 tablespoon of the sugar, and the warm water in the bowl of a standing mixer fitted with the dough hook, and let sit for 5 minutes, until foamy. In a medium mixing bowl, whisk together the eggs, remaining sugar, and salt. Turn the mixer on low, and pour the egg mixture over the yeast; mix until well combined, about 1 minute. Add 1½ cups of the flour, and mix until smooth. Add the melted butter, and mix well. Add the remaining 3 cups flour, 1 cup at a time, and mix until the dough has a smooth, elastic texture.

Lightly oil another large bowl. Place the dough in the bowl; turn to coat with oil. Cover the bowl with plastic wrap, then cover with a kitchen towel. Let the dough rise in a warm, draft-free area until doubled in volume, about 1½ hours (or, at this point, the dough can be refrigerated overnight, then rolled out and filled the next day).

Meanwhile, make the filling. Combine the softened butter, brown sugar, and cinnamon in a medium mixing bowl.

After the dough has risen, turn it out onto a lightly floured work surface, and roll it into a 12 × 15-inch rectangle (the size of a half-sheet tray). Using a rubber spatula, spread ½ cup of the butter mixture evenly over the dough. Sprinkle the butter with ½ cup of the pecans and the raisins. Starting with the long edge, roll the dough, jelly roll–style, into a large pinwheel cylinder. Cut the cylinder into nine equal rolls.

Lightly grease a 9 × 13-inch cake pan, then spread the remaining butter mixture evenly over the bottom of the pan and sprinkle with the remaining ½ cup pecans. Arrange the dough slices in staggered rows of three (pinwheel swirl-side down), three across and three down on top of the butter mixture. Press each dough piece lightly to spread into an even circle. The slices in the rows across should just touch; there will be a space between the rows down. Cover the pan with plastic wrap and allow the dough to rise in a warm, draft-free spot for 45 minutes to an hour, until the rolls have doubled in bulk.

Preheat the oven to 350°F.

Bake the rolls, uncovered, for 20 to 25 minutes, until the tops are golden brown. Remove the pan from the oven and cool for 5 minutes on a baking rack. Using a sharp knife, cut around the sides of pan. Place a large baking sheet over the pan. Using oven mitts, hold the baking sheet and pan together tightly and flip over, releasing the cinnamon rolls onto the baking sheet (use a rubber spatula to scrape any remaining buttery syrup or nuts onto the tops of the rolls). Serve the cinnamon rolls warm or at room temperature.

MAKES 9 LARGE ROLLS

Sorghum Molasses and Cane Syrup

BOTH SORGHUM MOLASSES and cane syrup are used as sweeteners throughout the South. Cane syrup, made from sugar cane, has a deeper, more bittersweet taste than sorghum molasses, which is made from the juice of sorghum stalks and tastes more like dark honey. Both sugar cane and sorghum thrive in the sweltering Southern climate, which is why both syrups remain popular there.

Fresh Blueberry Muffins

Gina: Everybody loves fresh blueberry muffins, and this recipe is the best one we've tried. The sugar topping adds a sweet crunch.

Twelve 2½-inch paper muffin-cup liners

8 tablespoons unsalted butter, at room temperature
1 cup plus 1 tablespoon granulated sugar
2 large eggs
1 teaspoon pure vanilla extract
½ cup sour cream
½ cup whole milk
2¼ cups all-purpose flour
2 teaspoons baking powder
½ teaspoon baking soda
½ teaspoon kosher salt
2½ cups fresh blueberries, picked through for stems
2 tablespoons light-brown sugar
½ teaspoon ground cinnamon

Preheat the oven to 350°F. Line a 12-cup muffin tin with paper liners.

In the bowl of an electric mixer fitted with the paddle attachment, cream the butter and 1 cup of the granulated sugar until light and fluffy, 2 to 3 minutes. With the mixer at low speed, add the eggs, one at a time, then add the vanilla, sour cream, and milk. In a separate bowl, sift together the flour, baking powder, baking soda, and salt. With the mixer at low speed, add the flour mixture to the batter, and beat until just mixed. Fold in the blueberries with a spatula, and be sure the batter is completely mixed.

In a small bowl, stir together the brown sugar, cinnamon, and remaining tablespoon of granulated sugar.

Scoop the batter into the prepared muffin tin, filling each cup just over the top, and bake for 10 minutes. Remove from the oven, sprinkle with the brown-sugar-and-cinnamon topping, and bake for another 10 to 15 minutes, until the muffins are lightly browned on top and a cake tester comes out clean.

MAKES 12 MUFFINS

Chocolate Chip Muffins

Gina: A muffin for the chocolate lover in all of us. They're great for festive brunches and holiday breakfasts, or with a cup for tea for an afternoon pick-me-up. Pat's been known to sneak them in the middle of the night, too, to eat with his ice cream (he thinks I'm not watchin', but, girlfriend, you know we are *always* watchin' . . .).

Twelve 2½-inch paper muffin-cup
    liners

1 cup all-purpose flour
1½ teaspoons baking powder
¼ teaspoon salt
8 tablespoons butter, melted
½ cup sugar
1 large egg
1 cup sour cream
2 teaspoons finely grated orange
    zest
1 teaspoon vanilla extract
1 cup semisweet mini–chocolate
    chips (7½ ounces)
1 cup chopped ripe banana
    (optional)

Preheat the oven to 400°F. Line a 12-cup muffin tin with paper liners.

In a medium bowl, whisk together the flour, baking powder, and salt. In another bowl, stir together the melted butter, sugar, egg, sour cream, orange zest, and vanilla. Stir the butter mixture into the flour mixture until just combined, then fold in the mini–chocolate chips and the banana, if using. Divide the batter among the muffin cups (this batter is thick and will not run easily, like other muffin batters), and bake in the middle of the oven until the tops are golden and a cake tester inserted in the center of a muffin comes out clean, about 20 minutes.

MAKES 12 MUFFINS

French Toast Panini with Grilled Bananas

Pat: French toast is one of my greatest loves. I like mine made with thick slices of white bread and a rich egg-and-milk batter with a kiss of cinnamon, and topped with lots of maple syrup. I also love to have a couple of over-easy eggs alongside. Gina is always saying to me, "Why you gotta fry eggs? There are eggs in the batter!"

Gina: I'm not sure if the French were the ones who made this toast famous, but I'm sure they would love what I've done to it: turned it into a sandwich! Everyone knows two pieces of French toast are better than one, and the only thing better than two pieces of French toast is two pieces with something sweet sandwiched in between! How about bananas? Then you take the whole thing and cook it on a panini press. The hot grill makes for an irresistibly crispy version of a morning classic, and it creates grooves that collect plenty of butter and maple syrup. You love peanut butter? Consider making a peanut-butter-banana French-toast sandwich. (Peanut butter was my protein staple during both my pregnancies.) The possibilities, girl, are endless. Bread that is a day or two old works best for this recipe, because it holds up better on the grill.

6 large eggs

1 cup whole milk

½ cup heavy cream

¼ cup fresh orange juice (from about 1 medium orange)

2 tablespoons pure vanilla extract

2 tablespoons cognac (optional)

2 tablespoons granulated sugar

½ teaspoon ground cinnamon

Pinch freshly grated nutmeg

Pinch salt

8 slices "Texas toast," or other white bread sliced 1 inch thick

3 large ripe bananas

2 tablespoons unsalted butter, melted

3 tablespoons vegetable oil or butter, for the panini grill

Confectioners' sugar, for garnish

Pure maple syrup

Whisk together the eggs, milk, cream, juice, vanilla, cognac, granulated sugar, cinnamon, nutmeg, and salt in a bowl; set aside.

Place the bread in a shallow baking dish large enough to hold the bread slices in a single layer. Pour the egg mixture over the bread, and soak for 10 minutes.

While the bread is soaking, heat a panini grill to high. Brush the bananas evenly with the melted butter. Place the bananas on the grill, lightly close the cover (do not press the cover down tightly or you'll have banana mush), and grill for about 3 minutes, until the bananas have nice grill marks and are beginning to release their juices. Use a spatula to transfer the bananas to a plate, then use a paper towel to wipe the panini grill clean. When the bananas are cool enough to handle, cut them into ½-inch-thick slices.

Preheat the oven to 200°F.

Remove a piece of bread from the egg mixture, allowing any excess moisture to drip off. Place the bread on a cutting board, top with four or five banana slices, then top with another piece of bread. Brush the panini grill lightly with vegetable oil, place the sandwich on the grill, press the top closed, and grill for 3 to 4 minutes, until crisp. Transfer the sandwich to a baking sheet, and keep warm in the oven while you grill the remaining sandwiches.

To serve, slice the panini in half diagonally, and serve warm with a dusting of confectioners' sugar and plenty of maple syrup on the side.

SERVES 6

MORE BREAKFAST PANINI

Consider making "sandwiches" with any of the following combos:

- Raspberries and mascarpone cheese
- Apple slices sautéed in butter and a sprinkling of sugar
- Cream cheese and apricot jam

Crunchy Pecan Waffles with Banana-Pecan Syrup and Strawberry Sauce

Gina: These delicious waffles are crispy, full of flavor, and loaded with crunchy pecans. You can serve them the traditional way, with syrup and butter, or jazz them up with sautéed bananas and/or fresh strawberry sauce. Either way, it's an unforgettable way to begin the day.

½ cup pecans

2 cups all-purpose flour

6 tablespoons light-brown sugar

1 teaspoon salt

2 teaspoons baking powder

1 teaspoon baking soda

1 teaspoon ground cinnamon

¼ teaspoon freshly grated nutmeg

4 large eggs, separated and at room temperature

6 tablespoons butter, melted, plus more for waffle iron

3 tablespoons cold butter

2 cups well-shaken buttermilk

1 teaspoon pure vanilla extract

⅛ teaspoon cream of tartar

1 cup pecan halves

2 bananas, sliced

1½ cups maple syrup

1 recipe Strawberry Sauce (recipe follows)

Preheat a waffle iron according to manufacturer's instructions, and preheat the oven to 200°F.

Place the pecans in the bowl of a food processor, and pulse until ground to the coarse size of small pebbles (do not grind them to a fine powder). Add the flour, brown sugar, salt, baking powder, baking soda, cinnamon, and nutmeg, and pulse until combined.

In a separate mixing bowl, whisk together the egg yolks, melted butter, buttermilk, and vanilla. Stir in the dry ingredients, and mix until incorporated—do not overmix.

Beat approximately one egg white and the cream of tartar with a hand mixer until foamy. Add the remaining whites and beat until stiff peaks appear. Fold the whites into the batter.

Brush the waffle iron with melted butter, or spray with nonstick cooking spray.

In a small sauté pan, heat the cold butter and the pecan halves. Cook, stirring occasionally, until the pecan halves are light golden and fragrant, 2 to 3 minutes. Add the banana slices, and sauté until light golden and soft, 2 to 3 minutes. Add the maple syrup, and bring to a simmer. Remove from the heat, and cover to keep warm.

Ladle the batter onto the waffle iron, and cook until golden brown, 3½ to 5 minutes. Repeat with the remaining batter, keeping the cooked waffles warm in the oven.

SERVES 4 TO 6

Strawberry Sauce

1 quart strawberries, hulled
  and sliced
¼ cup sugar
¼ cup water
1 teaspoon grated lemon zest
2 teaspoons fresh lemon juice
2 teaspoons cornstarch

In a small pot over medium heat, combine the strawberries, sugar, water, lemon zest, lemon juice, and cornstarch. Bring to a simmer, and stir gently until mixture thickens slightly.

MAKES ENOUGH FOR 4 TO 6 WAFFLES

Buttermilk Pancakes with Vanilla Bean–Berry Syrup

Pat: What suits a lazy, stay-in-your-pajamas kind of morning more than a stack of buttermilk pancakes topped with butter and a drizzle of spicy maple syrup? (Ours is infused with a fresh vanilla bean.) Aren't mornings grand?

Cornmeal gives these pancakes a toothsome appeal. If you want flavored pancakes, feel free to add a sprinkling of sliced bananas or peaches, shredded coconut, mini–chocolate chips, chopped toasted nuts, or granola to the batter. (You'll want to add nuts and granola to the pancakes after they have been poured onto the griddle—otherwise they will lose their crunch.)

1½ cups all-purpose flour
½ cup finely ground cornmeal
3 tablespoons granulated sugar
2 teaspoons baking powder
½ teaspoon salt
Pinch grated nutmeg
2¼ cups well-shaken buttermilk
2 large eggs, beaten
1 tablespoon vegetable oil, plus
    more for frying
Butter, for serving
1 recipe Vanilla Bean–Berry Syrup
    (recipe follows)
Confectioners' sugar, for garnish

Whisk together the flour, cornmeal, granulated sugar, baking powder, salt, and nutmeg in a large bowl. In a separate bowl, whisk together the buttermilk, eggs, and oil. Stir the wet ingredients into the dry ingredients, and stir just until blended, being careful not to overmix (a few lumps are okay). Cover the batter with plastic wrap, and chill for at least 1 hour and for up to 8 hours. If necessary, thin with water or extra buttermilk before cooking, being careful not to overbeat.

Heat a large skillet or griddle over medium-high heat. Add enough oil to grease it lightly and leave a film on the bottom of the pan.

Working in batches, ladle the batter, about ½ cup at a time, into the pan. Cook until the pancakes are golden brown and bubbles start to form on the top, about 1 minute per side. Flip the pancakes just as the surface bubbles begin to rise. (Flipping them after all the bubbles are gone produces a flatter pancake.) Transfer to a platter, and cover to keep warm while you make additional pancakes.

Divide the pancakes into stacks among four plates, placing a pat of softened butter between each of them, and pour warm Vanilla Bean–Berry Syrup over each stack. Sprinkle with confectioners' sugar, if desired.

SERVES 4

His and Her Margaritas

Gina: I love a little bit of whimsy, and what better time for that than when you are kicking back with your man enjoying a cocktail? I didn't think Pat would be too keen on sipping a pink drink, so I made his bright blue. Both variations are potent and delish, so just pick the flavor (or color) that suits your mood (or matches your shoes or your handbag . . .).

HERS

¼ cup kosher salt

¼ cup pink sanding sugar (see note)

2 ounces best-quality silver tequila (I like Patrón)

1 ounce Grand Marnier

2 ounces fresh lime juice

½ ounce grenadine

Lime wedges, for garnish

HIS

¼ cup kosher salt

¼ cup blue sanding sugar (see note)

2 ounces best-quality silver tequila (I like Patrón)

1 ounce blue Curaçao

1 ounce Grand Marnier

2 ounces fresh lime juice

Combine the salt and pink sanding sugar, and then the salt and blue sanding sugar, in two separate saucers. Fill another saucer with water. Dip the rim of each of two glasses in the water, then the salt-and-sugar to coat. Combine the ingredients for each cocktail into two separate cocktail shakers filled with ice. Shake well, and pour into the salt-and-sugar-rimmed cocktail glasses.

MAKES 2 POTENT DRINKS

NOTE: Sanding sugar has a slightly larger grain than granulated sugar, and it's got a great sparkle to it. It's available in assorted colors at baking supply stores, or online at, among other sites, www.kingarthurflour.com.

Lazy Sunday Mimosa

What can I say, girlfriends? It is not uncommon for my husband to serve me mimosas, along with breakfast in bed, on a Sunday morning. You think he's looking for something in return? I figure we work hard all week and he's just treating me special. I tell you what, though: Nothing kicks off a lazy, loving Sunday like a sip of bubbles. We make these drinks one at a time, allowing the shifting strawberries to mix the drink as you sip, but you could also combine the ingredients in a large serving pitcher.

½ cup pink sanding sugar (see note to preceding recipe)

6 to 8 fresh strawberries, stemmed and halved

One 750ml bottle brut champagne or Prosecco

Splash blood-orange juice, plus more as needed

1 tablespoon Grand Marnier, plus more as needed

Dip the rims of two or four champagne flutes in water. Dip in the sanding sugar. Drop several strawberry halves into each glass. Fill each glass about two-thirds with champagne, leaving room for a splash each of blood-orange juice and Grand Marnier. Serve immediately, and repeat as necessary.

SERVES 2 ON A LAZY SUNDAY
(OR 4 ON A MORE PRODUCTIVE ONE)

Girls' Night Martini

Gina: When I'm hanging with my girlfriends and we want something strong and sweet, this smooth, sexy cocktail, flavored with chocolate, coffee, and banana, does the trick. A splash of espresso gives us the fuel to stay awake for another round.

2 tablespoons turbinado sugar

2 tablespoons cocoa powder

4 tablespoons prepared espresso, cooled

1½ ounces best vodka, chilled

½ ounce crème de cacao

½ ounce banana schnapps

Chocolate swizzle sticks, for garnish (optional)

Moisten the rim of a chilled, oversized martini glass with water. Pour the sugar and cocoa into a saucer, and mix well. Dip the rim of the glass in the mixture, and roll to coat the rim thoroughly.

Combine the espresso, vodka, crème de cacao, and banana schnapps in a cocktail shaker, add a handful of ice, and shake until frothy. Strain into the prepared glass. Garnish with a chocolate swizzle stick, if desired, and look out.

MAKES 1 POTENT DRINK

Raspberry Iced Tea

Gina: You don't think my whimsy ends with cocktails, do you? Sweet iced tea is the elixir of the South, so I decided that our Neely "house" tea needed to have a little pizzazz. Honey, I found it by combining fresh raspberries with hibiscus tea, which has a brilliant crimson color and beautiful fruit-and-floral flavors.

---

10 bags Raspberry Zinger tea
4 bags hibiscus tea
12 cups water

SUGAR SYRUP
1 cup sugar
1 cup water
1 pint raspberries

½ cup fresh lime juice
Fresh mint sprigs, for garnish

Place the tea bags in a large heat-proof pitcher. Boil the water, pour it over the tea bags, and allow it to steep for at least 10 minutes. Remove the tea bags, and allow the tea to cool.

Combine the sugar and water in a small saucepan, and bring the mixture to a boil. Reduce the heat and simmer briefly, stirring, until the sugar is dissolved. Remove from the heat and add the raspberries, then allow the mixture to come to room temperature.

Combine the tea, raspberry syrup, and fresh lime juice in a large pitcher. To serve, pour the sweet tea into large glasses filled with ice and garnish with sprigs of mint.

SERVES 8

Fresh Peach Sangria

Gina: This light-colored sangria, made with white wine, is as beautiful as it is refreshing and delicious. You can make and serve this drink immediately, but it's even better if you can prepare it in advance, so the fruit flavors have a chance to permeate the wine.

2 bottles dry white wine (such as Pinot Grigio or sauvignon blanc), chilled

½ cup brandy

1 cup pineapple juice

½ cup superfine sugar

4 peaches, pitted and sliced

2 red or black plums, pitted and sliced

2 cups green grapes, halved

1 lemon, sliced into rounds

Combine the wine, brandy, pineapple juice, sugar, peaches, plums, grapes, and lemon slices in a large pitcher, and stir until the sugar is dissolved. Add ice cubes to fill and serve immediately, or refrigerate for up to 1 day in advance and add ice cubes before serving.

SERVES 6 TO 8

Peabody Mint Julep

The grand lobby of the Peabody Hotel in Memphis is called "the living room of the South," for good reason. It's the best spot in town to sink into a comfy lounge chair, sip a cocktail, and watch people, or the occasional parade of ducks, come and go. Their bracing mint julep is justifiably famous.

⅓ cup water
⅔ cup sugar, plus more for garnish
2 bunches fresh mint leaves, roughly torn and bruised, plus additional sprigs for garnish
One 750ml bottle Maker's Mark whiskey

Bring the water, sugar, and mint leaves to a boil in a medium saucepan. Reduce the heat and simmer briefly, stirring, until the sugar dissolves completely. Cool the syrup completely, then strain it into a large pitcher. Add the whiskey, and stir to combine. Serve immediately in chilled julep glasses with crushed ice and fresh sprigs of mint, for garnish. You can also return the whiskey/syrup mixture to the empty whiskey bottle and freeze overnight. It will freeze to a nice slushy consistency for serving on scorching afternoons.

SERVES A CROWD

"Beale Street" Jack Daniel's Lemonade

You can use regular lemonade to make this Southern refresher, but we like to use the tart Italian Limonata made by San Pellegrino (it's available in most grocery stores).

2 ounces Jack Daniel's whiskey
One 12-ounce can San Pellegrino Limonata (or ½ cup lemonade concentrate, thawed, plus ¼ cup seltzer)
2 teaspoons Maraschino cherry juice
Maraschino cherries, for garnish

Pour the whiskey, half of the Limonata (or all of the lemonade concentrate and seltzer), and the Maraschino cherry juice into a cocktail shaker with crushed ice. Shake well to combine, and divide the mixture between two highball glasses. Add the remaining Limonata and garnish with a Maraschino cherry.

MAKES 2 DRINKS

Midnight Chocolate Malt

Pat: My weakness for ice cream is well known, and the name of this drink says it all: This is the kind of decadent concoction that you whip up in the middle of the night, when you can raid the freezer, the fruit bowl, and your daughters' candy stash and no one is the wiser. Just in case the blender wakes up your wife (or kids), this recipe makes enough for two.

1 pint premium chocolate ice cream
¾ cup coffee-flavored liqueur
   (we use Kahlúa)
¼ cup whole milk (more if
   necessary)
3 tablespoons chocolate syrup
1 ripe banana
4 tablespoons malt powder
1 cup chocolate-covered malt balls
   (I recommend Whoppers)

Combine the ice cream, liqueur, milk, chocolate syrup, and banana in a blender and process on low speed for 30 seconds, until smooth (add more milk if necessary to dilute the mixture). Add the chocolate-covered malt balls, and process for another 20 seconds. Pour into two tall glasses, and serve with a spoon (if you're lucky, it will be too thick for a straw).

SERVES 2 SLEEPWALKERS

Acknowledgments

Pat: Gina and I are so grateful for all the support from our fans, family members, and friends. You guys mean the world to us, and this book would not have been possible without your encouragement, patience, and love.

In addition, we would like to thank the following people:

Jonathan Russo at Artists Agency for your energy and encouragement throughout this entire journey. We have many great projects ahead.

Janis Donnaud, our literary agent, you are a true professional. From the first time I met you, I knew we were in great hands.

Paul Bogaards, Sheila O'Shea, and the entire Knopf team, we are so happy to have worked with you on this project. Your experience helped us write a book that we are truly proud of.

Paula Deen, you have been like a second mother to Gina and me. You took us under your wing and mentored, supported, and encouraged us. You are what we in the South call our "Play Mama." We love you, and "Thank you very much."

Paula Disbrowe, you did it! You helped us produce a book we will always treasure. I'm so proud to know you and to have worked with you on our first book, and I'm excited about the prospect of our future collaborations.

Gordon Elliot and Mark Schneider, our producers at Follow Productions, you are true friends. When we first met you, we didn't know what to expect. You told us we had a story to tell and you helped us tell it. You had a vision for us, and that vision has become a reality. Thank you for believing, and for seeing something in us that no one else saw. We love you both.

The entire Neely's Bar-B-Que family, you have been and continue to be our frontline soldiers, holding our business together and taking care of our customers while Gina and I travel the country and work on our books and TV shows.

My dear aunt Faye, your strength and love mean so much to Gina and me. We love you. Thank you.

My brothers Mark and Gaelin, we are, and always will be, one. Your words and hard work will never be taken for granted. I love you. Thank you.

My brother Tony, I can't put on paper what our relationship means to me. We have been to hell and back, and *thank God* we made it back. None of this would have been possible without you. I could not ask for a better big brother. You are a "true brother" in every sense. Your support has been incredible, and Lord knows where I'd be without you. *THANK YOU VERY MUCH.*

My momma, Lorine, my rock through the years. You always put your children first. You never gave up on me, on any of us. You were the first one to put a pot in my hand and say to me, "You can cook." All those years that you spent with me in the kitchen paid off. Without a mother like you, I don't know where I would be. I hope you are proud of how things turned out. God knows I'd be lost without you.

My dear, beautiful wife, Gina—my love for you sustains me. From the first time we met, I knew you were special, and writing this book with you reminded me how lucky I am to have found my "first love" and to still be with her! Not many people can say that. You, Spenser, and Shelbi are the biggest joys in my life and the reason this book is possible. I would not be the cook I am today, and certainly there would be no *Down Home with the Neelys* without you and our beautiful daughters. You make me happy. Spenser and Shelbi, I love you with all my heart, soul, and life. I will never stop trying to "steal your sugar." THANK YOU, THANK YOU, THANK YOU.

—PAT NEELY

Gina: First and foremost, I want to *thank God* for giving Pat and me an opportunity to share our love and passion. Never in a million years would I have guessed that God would choose us to share a message of love and empowerment with others. It has been an amazing journey, overwhelming in some ways, educational in others, and blessed by spiritual growth.

I thank God for allowing Mark Schneider and Gordon Elliot, and the entire family at Follow Productions, to sense something in our blessings. They thought people would identify with our story. I guess they were right. Gordon and Mark have become family, and, *honey, that ain't easy*! *Thank you* for believing in us. Thanks, Gordon, for introducing us to Paula Deen. Paula, you're an exceptional woman who overcame so much—talk about "Girl Power." Thanks, Paula, for pulling me aside and saying, "Sometimes God blesses us in ways that we can't imagine. Allow it to happen." I was so *afraid* of this blessing—you guys can't even imagine. It's so funny that people tell me I look so at ease, because early on I was a mess!

This book owes a huge debt to the wonderful people who have supported us from the beginning and assisted us in telling our story.

Jonathan Russo, thank you for all you do. Your insight on this project has taught us so much, and your guidance and support means the world to us.

Janis Donnaud, thanks so much for your direction and for "keeping it real" when necessary. You helped us more than you know.

Paul Bogaards, Sheila O'Shea, and the entire Knopf family, this opportunity and experience has been so much fun. Your help with this book gave us the mojo to see it through to the end. Better stop here before I write another love letter!

Paula Disbrowe, "Miss Thang," you can bring a story to life! Are you sure you're not my sistah? I have met some wonderful women on this journey. Thanks to our family at Food Network, especially Ronnie Weinstock (thank you for kicking my butt in such a nice way that I didn't even know you kicked it!).

To my girls, Spenser and Shelbi, I love you. Thank you for supporting me when you didn't even realize it, and for jumping on the bandwagon when none of us even knew the tune.

To my mom, Jean Ervin, my first and number one fan. Thank you for pushing, pushing, and pushing me. I didn't understand it then, but I am clear about it now (and now I am pushing my girls in just the same way. See, ladies, we really do become our mothers!). Thank you for giving me my first example of tenacity, strength, and endurance—I love you! Thanks to my immediate family: Ronnie (big brother, substitute dad, spiritual partner), Kim (second mom and motivator), Tanya (my silent, supportive partner in crime), and Jackie (keepin' it real, sistah). To my incredible village (too many to name but you know who you are), where would I be without you all?

To my lovable, understanding, workaholic, strong, gorgeous, and great-provider-of-a-man, better known as *BIG DADDY*. Patrick, you are an incredible husband, and you've been the most wonderful father to our girls. I never guessed this would happen, but God knew all along.

Last but not least, thank you, fans! You guys support me when I'm looking a mess, looking fabulous, and not looking at all. You cannot imagine what your kind words do for me.

—GINA NEELY

Index

Page references in *italics* refer to illustrations.